Afrikan Alphabets

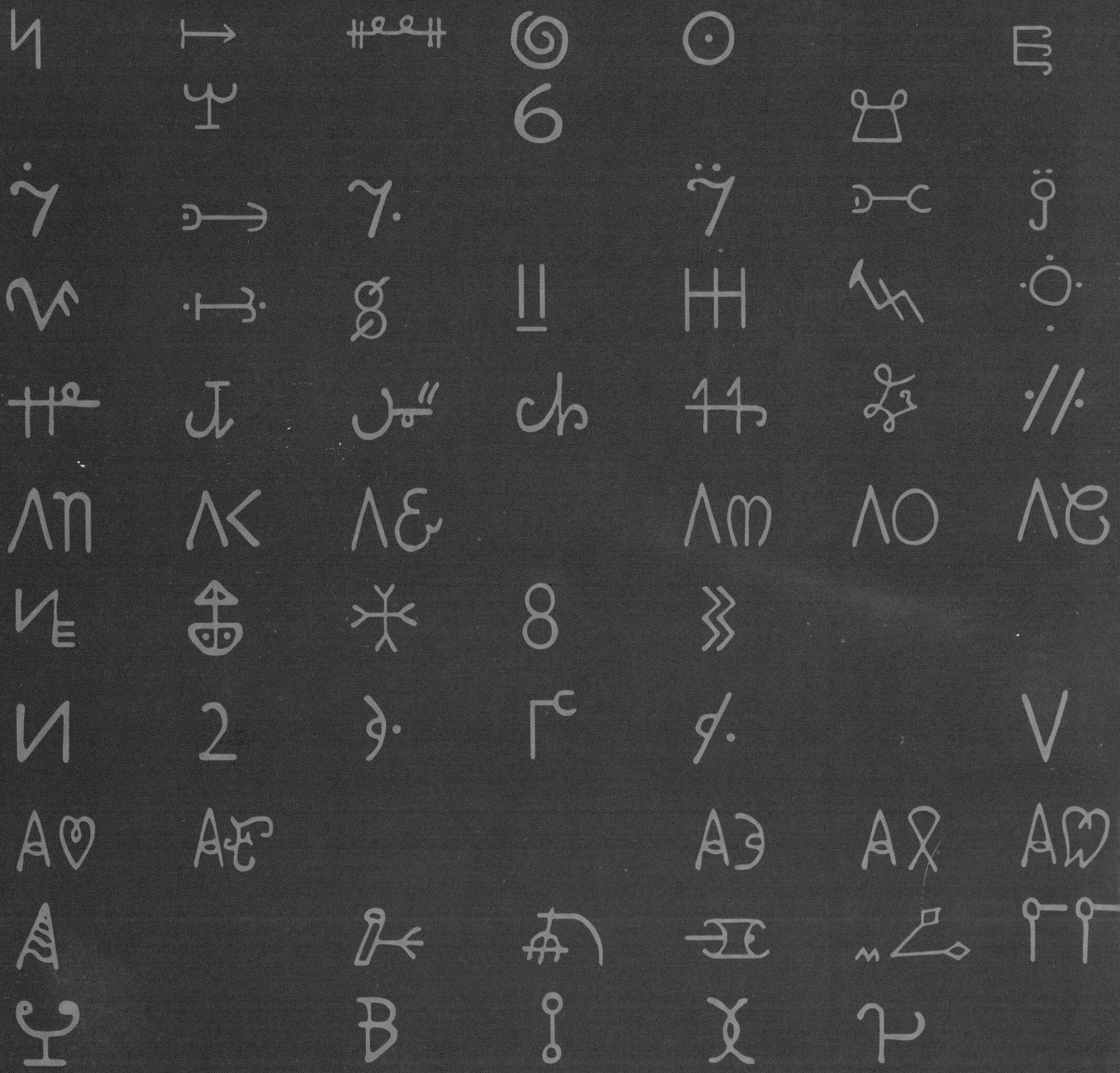

Afrikan Alphabets

The story of writing in Afrika

Mark Batty Publisher

SAKI MAFUNDIKWA

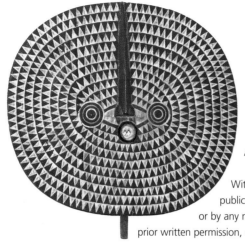

Bwa mask, Burkina Faso
Wood, pigment

Frontispiece: Each vertical column displays a different Afrikan alphabet shown in this book, each horizontal column shows the same syllable for each of the alphabets. Gaps denote unavailable syllables in some alphabets.

Afrikan Alphabets
Copyright © 2007 Saki Mafundikwa
The preface for this edition © Maurice Tadadjeu
Book design by Saki Mafundikwa
All photography by the author except where noted otherwise.

Every effort has been made to trace accurate ownership of copyrighted text and visual material used in this book. Errors or omissions will be corrected in subsequent editions, provided notification is sent to the publisher. Credits and acknowledgements are continued on page 149.

Library of Congress Control Number: 2003112063

Printed and bound at the National Press, Hashemite Kingdom of Jordan

First Paperback Edition
10 9 8 7 6 5 4 3 2 1

This edition © 2007
Mark Batty, Publisher
36 W 37th St, Penthouse
New York, NY 10018 USA
www.markbattypublisher.com

ISBN: 0-9772827-6-7

Great men make history,
but only such history as it is possible for them to make.
Their freedom of achievement is limited by the necessities of their environment.
To portray the limits of those necessities
and the realization, complete or partial, of all possibilities,
that is the true business of the historian.

—C.L.R. James in **The Black Jacobins**

For my boyz,
Tichakunda and Simba
whom I plucked away from Brooklyn for Harare
so they could grow up knowing who they are.

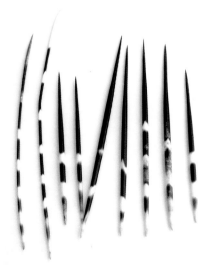

Contents

Nwantantay mask
(reverse, at left and front on facing page)
Bwa people, Burkina Faso
Wood, pigment
16.25 x 72 x 10 inches (41.28 x 182.9 x 25.4 cm)
Nwantantay – great plank mask primarily used from March until early May,
when the rains begin. Like alphabets, the patterns on such masks are more than
decorations and combine to convey stories and represent abstract concepts
and complex thoughts.

The African Art Museum of the SMA Fathers, Tenafly, NJ
Gift of Steward J. Warkow, 1998
Photo: Tapiwa Muronda

Preface

What is the point in writing the name Africa in English with a **k**? What is the difference between *Africa* and *Afrika*? Obviously one difference is in the visual appearance of the two spellings of the same name. The two sound identical but look different.

It was not until I met the author of this book, Saki Mafundikwa, that such a difference became rather embarrassing to me. In fact, I cannot recall any African language that spells *Africa* with a **c**. *Africa* is spelt *Afrika* in African languages. I should confess right away that, I am confused as I write this preface. Something deep inside me tells me that Saki is right in writing *Africa* with a **k**. At the same time, I feel that I am bound by my habit inherited from English, to continue spelling that name with a **c**, in order to be consistent with myself and with the English writing tradition. So I am not yet as free as Saki in changing the spelling of this name. At first glance, this may appear trivial. But it is not. As you read this book, you will discover that this is a fundamental issue which is part of African identity and reflected in the writing systems devised by Africans over the centuries for their own languages.

African writing systems are not the sole symbols of African identity. My book entitled *Voie Africaine* (*The African Way of Life*) suggests that the African common currency should be called AFRI: the first four letters, which are found in the same order, in the spelling of the name Africa, in all written languages. This proposal is still valid today, especially as the European Union

Characters of Shü-mom
The syllabary invented in 1902 by King Ibrahim Njoya of the Bamum people of Cameroon so that the Bamum would be able to record their history and literature in their own language with their own script. See page 82.

came up years later with the same proposal for EURO, which is already operational. Currency is one of the most powerful symbols of identity. The name of a currency, like that of a country, a place or a person, can be neither chosen nor spelt haphazardly.

Logically, non-African languages should take the spelling of African names from African languages. It can be argued that writing systems in African languages have been too limited in number and in circulation to be able to influence the spelling of Africa in non-African languages. Such an argument is not fully satisfactory and the reason for this is part of the story told in this book.

Many authors, with varying emphasis on particular aspects, have told the story of African writing systems. This book presents an informal review and emphasizes the graphic aspects. The author is a graphic designer by profession. Designers in general and African designers in particular have African writing systems as immense sources of inspiration. But designers are not the only professionals to benefit from this book. Linguists in general, and developers of African language writing systems in particular, stand to reap the fruit of this enduring research. Most linguists have not felt much concern about reviving the old writing systems of African languages; the issue of the practical usefulness of these systems remains open to debate. Nevertheless, the study of old African language writing systems, devised by genuine African inventors, should become a required discipline in linguistics departments throughout African universities. I should like to take the case of the Shü-mom writing system in Cameroon to illustrate this point.

In February 1985, a colloquium was organized in the city of Foumban (western province of Cameroon) as part of the celebration of the centenary anniversary of the Bamum Royal Palace. I had the honor of presenting to the panel of scholars gathered on that occasion a linguistic assessment of the Shü-mom writing system, invented by King Njoya, at the dawn of the 20th century.

My paper clearly established that this writing system fulfilled the scientific criteria for a complete, coherent and functional writing system, which could be used to write any human language. This was also, for me, a unique occasion in which I was privileged to pay a personal homage to King Njoya as the very first Cameroonian linguist, and in fact, the most illustrious among us all. Although he had never sat in any linguistic course, he had been able to achieve in the Shü-mom language what we are now devoting our scholarly careers to do, namely, developing writing systems for unwritten African languages.

With the participation of some 3,000 linguists across the continent, I have since developed a project to put into writing all the unwritten languages of Africa. This project will be completed during the first two decades of the 21st century. In this endeavor, the graphic representation of the sounds found specifically in African languages is a crucial concern. My encounter with the author of this book was a delightful occasion, which highlighted our common interest in graphic representation in general and particularly as it applies to the writing of African languages.

In this book, Saki goes far and freely beyond the writing systems of African languages to touch on several related issues. One issue is funding research on African languages, cultures, and graphic systems. I want to say a word on this specific financial aspect because I feel that there is a general solution to it. Africans should not expect other peoples to significantly fund the promotion of African languages and cultures. Africa has sufficient human and natural resources on which to draw to revive and develop African cultures. African civil society has come up with an interesting proposal in this regard.

The idea is that the newly established African Union should institute a continental income tax to finance major projects with a continent-wide impact. This would be a contribution of 6% of the annual income of Africans on the continent and in the Diaspora, and of African public and private enterprises and foreign enterprises established on the continent. In addition, a contribution of 15% of State revenue from the exploitation of national natural resources would constitute an important contribution to the financial resources of the African Union. Such an income tax system would generate billions of dollars annually for investment in major continental projects, such as NEPAD (New Partnership for Africa's Development) projects.

It should be recalled that Africa, in fact, is not poor. This continent is endowed with immense natural and human resources. It is paradoxical that the exploitation of such resources should result in the current abject poverty of the continent's people. The above proposal is a real and feasible solution to this paradoxical problem.

I would not feel so embarrassed about writing the name Africa in English with a **k** if I was still not so limited in financial resources to promote the generalization of such a spelling – which actually reflects African identity. After all, we have seen African countries such as Benin, Burkina Faso, and Zimbabwe change their names. We are seeing more and more Africans on the continent and in the Diaspora change their names and adopt the names that reflect what they feel is their real identity. These are all State and individual decisions that have costs attached to them. Once these costs are paid, these decisions are implemented accordingly.

Africa has the potential capacity to pay the price to reinforce her identity. It is the responsibility of the present generation of African leaders, intellectuals, civil society and the business community to pay the appropriate price to restore knowledge in Africa's long and rich cultural history, its unique identities, and its dignity. African communities have and will continue to achieve much. African writing systems are an important key to unlocking this huge potential.

Think about this as you read this book.

Maurice Tadadjeu, Ph.D.
Professor of African Languages and Linguistics
Yaoundé University
Yaoundé, Cameroon

Author's Introduction

Without the written word there would be no graphic design. The letters and symbols we write with are extremely important to a visual communicator like me. For people to write in the languages of their cultures is also important. That is the key reason why I undertook this book, to show how writing systems have evolved in Afrika and are still evolving today. This book is about writing systems. In its pages you will find more than a dozen different writing systems identified, defined, and discussed. This book is of necessity a summary: it seeks to say a little about each of these writing systems, and also to put these in a wider context of geography, history, and culture. It is intended to be accessible and to entertain as much as it informs.

I am a graphic designer and design educator and my specialty is typography. Designers communicate ideas and messages using both type and images. This used to be done mainly with print on paper, but now, with the advent of New Media, designers design for a virtual space: the computer screen. This is quite exciting for a typographer like me. Words on a screen can be given new emphasis that was not possible before on paper. Type can be used more expressively than ever before. Among the most expressive of graphic symbols are those created by Afrikans.

The purpose of this book is to provide an introduction to information in uncharted places about Afrikan alphabets. In this book I will only scratch the surface of this area of research. Afrika's deserts, rain forests, and savannas are rich with information yet to be discovered; so much research is waiting to be done. Afrikan alphabets are a way of expressing ideas, systems of thought, thought processes, cultural imperatives, aesthetic preferences, and spirit. Afrikan alphabets are one of the important keys to help unlock what has been kept hidden from so many for so long: that these alphabets with their deeply meaningful graphic construction show the intelligence and ingenuity of Afrikan peoples.

Before we go much further, especially for the growing number of grammatologists out there, let me clear up any confusion that might be caused by the title I chose for this book: *Afrikan Alphabets*. This book deals with the pictographs, ideographs, and scripts – mostly syllabaries – which were devised and designed by Afrikans.

A pictograph is a graphic character used in symbol writing. The symbolic picture represents an object or action. Examples of present-day pictographs are the universal male and female pictures that indicate the men's or women's restroom, or the human figure in mid-step on crossing signals alerting pedestrians that it is safe to walk.

An ideograph is a character or symbol representing an idea or concept without indicating the pronunciation of a particular word. The skull and crossbones on a bottle's label warns of poisoning, or the © means that someone holds legal rights to an idea or product, and ÷ means a particular mathematical operation.

A syllabary is a set of written characters, each character representing a single uninterrupted voice sound. For example, my last name, Mafundikwa, has four syllables – Ma-fun-dik-wa. By contrast, alphabetic systems rely on letters that by themselves are pure abstractions of sound. A single letter represents neither a syllable of sound, nor an idea. An alphabet is a system of letters or characters representing the individual sound elements of spoken language, usually containing consonants and vowels. My last name has 10 units of sound: m-a-f-u-n-d-i-k-w-a.

While alphabets tend to be small, syllabaries can be quite large: Most syllabaries are huge in their early development, when the symbol more often represents an entire word or idea. Some syllabaries started out with hundreds of characters, but their users frequently managed to cut them down to a few dozen, creating phonetic syllabaries. Afrikan alphabets are not all alphabets in the truest sense of the word. There were some Afrikan societies that devised actual alphabets that correspond well to the above definition, such as Tifinagh (page 47) and N'ko (page 131); other societies devised syllabaries, such as Mende (page 70) and Shü-mom (page 86).

The European colonizers claimed Afrikan territory with impunity, and thereby created new historical realities for the colonized. I have taken a cue from them and claimed the word *alphabet*; so for the title of this book, all writing systems become *alphabets* – hence, *Afrikan Alphabets*.

In Afrika the harmony of art, nature, and spirit is the rule, not the exception. In terms of the graphic arts, Afrikan alphabets show that the spiritual line is free and unencumbered by the rule of the grid. It relies on a natural freedom and fluidity. White space around the letters gives way to pattern that describes the fundamental truth of nature's own underlying shapes.

Afrikan alphabets are products of over more than 5,000 years of activity (although, perversely, much of this activity was not recorded for posterity until the last 200 years). The development of alphabets is not tied to political borders, or to a single people, but rather reflects the ebb and flow of peoples across a vast landmass. This has led to influences from other cultures, whether they are from within Afrika or from other continents. The influences include religious proselytizing, both Islamic and Christian; the pressure from colonizing forces from Europe; and commercial pressures, including the transatlantic slave trade.

In response to these influences, Afrikan peoples have sought to protect their diversity and keep confidences among themselves. Their alphabets are among the tools that have given Afrikans the means to maintain their cultures, arts, and religions.

A good designer, in Western terms, is one who knows type – mainly the Roman alphabet. It would seem that the Roman alphabet is the most widely used writing system in the world. But of course this is simply not so, since many more people use Arabic and Chinese writing systems than use the Roman alphabet.

Even very recently, students from all over the world would converge on the campuses of Europe and North America to learn graphic design. They would have to forget everything they knew about their own writing and learn the Roman alphabet (very fast!). While in college in the United States, I used to hear some of my instructors heap praise on students from Japan for being gifted designers. Well, all that is necessary is to look at Japanese writing to see how design is an integral part, in the same way old Chinese scrolls show a sense of layout with the texts arranged in grids. Design permeates all aspects of Japanese life, not just graphics but architecture, product design, industrial design, fashion, and even garden design.

Today, interest in design has led graphic artists from every corner of the globe to work in their native writing systems. Designers who have studied in the West changed the design landscape by redrawing and digitizing their writing systems, making them widely available through software for personal computers. Lack of knowledge about, and lack of access to materials relating to the creation of Afrikan alphabets has, until only very recently, hampered this digital translation for these alphabets.

There have always been voices speaking of Afrika's achievements both on the continent and in the West. In the United States they call themselves Afrocentrists. When Afrocentrist scholars first came on the scene in the 1980s, they were accused of romanticizing their Afrikan past. Some labeled them revisionists. Some critics of Afrocentrism, like former U.S. Secretary of Education William Bennett, believed Afrocentrism to be anti-American and a mistake. "It will further alienate the poor, who are already tenuously connected to American culture. It's a mistake to think these kids are going to get any more interested in school by studying more about Africa."

Professor Molefe Kete Asante of Temple University corrects Dr. Bennett's stance when he says: "Afrocentricity is both theory and practice. In its theoretical aspect it consists of interpretation and analysis from the perspective of African people as subjects rather than objects of the European experience. This

Stereotypes of Afrikan people in America as "Sambos" persisted well into the nineties. I bought this box of toothpaste in Chinatown, New York City, in 1991. Colgate Palmolive made this toothpaste for their Asian market. Afrikan-Americans protested and threatened to boycott their products in the U.S.; in response, Colgate " redesigned" the packaging – leaving the colors and the typography the same but changing the name to "Darlie" and the "Sambo" character to a sanitized and less offensive gender and race ambiguous character.

is not an idea to replace all things European, but to expand the dialogue to include African-American information." Professor Asante's approach is that recent Afrikan-American history has shown a pattern of imitation of European culture. More importantly, Afrikans, wherever they are, need to learn from their own cultural traditions as well. He poses the following question: How many Afrikan-Americans know the names of any of the Afrikan ethnic groups that were brought to the Americas during the Great Enslavement? Afrikan-Americans may have learned European ethnic names, but not these Afrikan names, because Afrikan-Americans have had so little exposure to their own Afrikan historical traditions.

The situation on the Afrikan continent, for the most part, is not that much different: most curricula still do not put Afrika at the center. Most history books still toe the colonial line of European supremacy. Someday, Afrika's story shall be told by her sons and daughters and all shall hear it. Afrikan alphabets are an important part of that story.

This book is intended to be a journey into little-charted areas of information, and I invite you to share this journey with me. I set out twenty years ago, and my journey has taken me from Harare to Havana; London to Lagos; Buckingham Palace in London to the Bamum Royal Palace in Foumban, Cameroon, and back again. It has straddled peoples, religions, cultures, educational systems, and beliefs. The journey has often been challenging but extremely rewarding. I have learned a lot about who I am along the way. If this book helps you to take away even a slight sense of the brilliant and independent thinking minds that made Afrikan alphabets, then I will have succeeded.

North & Northwestern Afrika :
Tifinagh (Morocco, Algeria, Libya, Niger, Mali, Burkino Faso)

Northern East Afrika:
Nuba Body Painting (Sudan)
Ethiopic
Somali Script

Western Afrika:
Aroko
Akan Gold Weights
Adinkra
Mande Syllabaries
Nsibidi/Anaforuana
Bassa (Vah) Alphabet
Djuka
N'ko Alphabet
Artist's/Poet's systems

Central Afrika:
Ishango Bone
Shü-mom Syllabary (Cameroon)

Southern Afrika:
Rock Art
Bantu Symbol Writing

Afrikan alphabets exist throughout the Afrikan continent. The names of writing systems are shown near their points of origin.

MOROCCO
TUNISIA
WESTERN SAHARA
ALGERIA
LIBYA
EGYPT
CAPE VERDE
MAURITANIA
MALI
NIGER
CHAD
SUDAN
ERITREA
DJIBOUTI
SENEGAL
GAMBIA
GUINEA BISSAU
GUINEA
BURKINO FASO
BENIN
GHANA
TOGO
NIGERIA
CENTRAL AFRICAN REPUBLIC
ETHIOPIA
SOMALIA
SIERRA LEONE
IVORY COAST
LIBERIA
CAMEROON
EQUATORIAL GUINEA
SAO TOME & PRINCIPE
GABON
CONGO
DEMOCRATIC REPUBLIC OF THE CONGO
UGANDA
RWANDA
BURUNDI
KENYA
SEYCHELLES
TANZANIA
ANGOLA
ZAMBIA
MALAWI
COMOROS
ZIMBABWE
MOZAMBIQUE
MAURITIUS
MADAGASCAR
NAMIBIA
BOTSWANA
SWAZILAND
LESOTHO
SOUTH AFRICA

My Journey

My own journey to tell this story began in the spring of 1983, as I was being interviewed for admission into the MFA program at the Yale School of Art.

"So, what language do you speak in Zimbabwe?" Alvin Eisenman, the head of the Graphic Design department, asked me.

"Shona," I replied.

"Is it a written language?"

"Why, of course, yes!"

"Wow, really? What are the characters like?" asked Professor Eisenman.

"Characters? You mean the letters? It's the Roman alphabet."

"No, I mean, do the Shona have their own writing system?"

"Writing system, what do you mean?" I asked.

"I have heard that some Afrikan societies have developed their own scripts, some of which are in existence today." Professor Eisenman told me.

"Really? Hmm, I'll have to look into that."

And look into it I did. I became a part of the design program at Yale and my master's thesis was called "Writing Systems in Afrikan Societies." I was encouraged to publish it "as is," but I felt more research, especially in the field in Afrika, needed to be done. Twenty years later, almost to the day, I finally feel ready to share my story, Afrika's story about alphabets, with you.

Interest in Afrikan writing systems has increased in the past twenty years, though mainly in academic circles. The general public still remains unaware

1

of the existence of Afrikan writing systems – which is a great loss. A most revealing view of Afrikan history emerges when contrasted with the circumstances surrounding the discovery of these systems and their fate in the hands of the colonizers. The out-of-date attitude that Afrikan writing systems are primitive and unsophisticated is being superseded by the realization that Afrikan letterforms reflect the artistic genius of some Afrikan peoples. The scholar John Henrik Clarke observed, "It is clear that the old concepts about Africa and the African people will die hard, but they will die."

I have concluded that the task of telling my own story cannot be truly successful without a process of complete de-colonization – a freeing of the self from mental slavery, an affliction rampant among many of us who were once colonized.

Colonialism succeeded for centuries by manufacturing a new elite among the residents of the colonized country. Middle-aged bureaucrats and missionaries would select a few bright adolescents to educate in the ways of the colonizers. Language was one of the most powerful weapons used against colonized Afrikan people. By teaching the young to speak English, French, or German the colonial masters strengthened their hold over the next generation. Jean-Paul Sartre describes this process as whitewashing. "The European elite undertook to manufacture a native elite. They picked out promising adolescents; they branded them, as with a red-hot iron, with the principles of Western culture; they stuffed their mouths full with high-sounding phrases, grand glutinous words that stuck to the teeth. After a short stay in the mother country they were sent home, whitewashed." I remember asking a fellow Afrikan student at Yale if he knew of the writing systems of his people. He looked at me puzzled, his face creased with annoyance, and wondered aloud, "Why are you interested in that stuff? It is only of interest to the backward people deep in the countryside."

There are other stories of Afrikans overcoming the colonized minds of their youth. As Malidoma Patrice Somé of the Dagara says about his life story: "The story I am going to tell comes from a place deep inside myself, a place that perceives all that I have irremediably lost and, perhaps, what gain there is behind the loss. If some people forget their past as a way to survive, other people remember it for the same reason." In his book *Of Water and the*

Spirit, Somé recounts his abduction and education at a Jesuit mission in the 1950s. When he finally escapes from the priests and returns home to Burkina Faso, he finds himself a stranger among his own people, the Dagara. "Exile creates the ideal conditions for an inventory of the warehouse of one's past," he notes. Once home, he has to re-learn the Dagara language because at the Jesuit school he had been forced to communicate only in French. Somé's beautifully told autobiography describes his adaptation to a culture with which he no longer had kinship. The village elders are suspicious of him because he has acquired the ways of the white man, mostly the ability to write. Soon enough, however, they all come to him for help in writing letters to their sons who had left for the city looking for employment and "a better life."

Fela strikes a characteristically dramatic and defiant pose.

Photo by Femi Bankole Onsula

The Afrikan continent does not lack her own soldiers. Many revolutionaries have fought (and most who have died) for emancipation from the shackles of imperialism. Political leaders like Kwame Nkrumah, Amil Cabral, Patrice Lumumba, Thomas Sankara, Steve Biko – the list is long. There are others as well, like the legendary Nigerian musician, creator, and avatar of Afrobeat, Fela Anikulapo Kuti.

With his superlative band (Afrika 70, later Egypt 80) Fela single-mindedly led a musical onslaught on imperialism, colonization, and the injustice meted out by repressive and corrupt Afrikan governments. He spared no one. His songs include assaults on mindless and violent soldiers, "Zombie"; on greedy and dishonest multinational corporations, "ITT – International T'ief T'ief"; on presidents, "Coffin for Head of State"; on the petit bourgeoisie living in splendor, oblivious to people living in squalor right next door, "Ikoyi Blindness." Fela's rapid-fire lyrics were delivered unapologetically in pidgin English, the language spoken by the ordinary people of Nigeria. His shows featured two or three songs, each over an hour long. A renegade and nonconformist, he once stopped the music after a single long song at a show I attended in New York to announce that he was not going to continue with the show until he was paid in full by the promoter of the concert. The crowd hissed and booed the promoter. Fela started to tell jokes and folk stories from his Nigerian childhood. Suddenly a voice from the back shouted "MUSIC!" Fela responded tauntingly, "Music? I can tell by the accent you are one of those colonized Nigerians!" Class differences among Nigerians was immediately evident to Fela, who himself had a privileged upbringing. The great singer loathed the colonial habits that persist among his countrymen.

At another show in Lagos in the seventies, according to *New York Times* reporter John Darnton, Fela admonished his audience to throw away their toothbrushes, which he saw as a vestige of colonialism. "Before the white man came, we Africans used sharpened sticks to clean our teeth," said Fela, glaring out from the stage. "I've thrown away my toothbrush. My brothers, we must all throw away our toothbrushes!"

I agree with Fela that Afrikans need to craft intellectual toothpicks of their own, reflecting Afrikan tradition and culture, to enable the removal of the grand glutinous words Sartre saw decaying the teeth of the Afrikan mind. This is the only way progress can be made towards total emancipation. This is why it was important for me to visit the cities and villages of Afrika for stories of Afrikan alphabets, rather than just the libraries of America and Europe.

I was able to get to West Afrika in January 2003 to carry out my research, but because of the civil war in Liberia, I was not able to study the Vai alphabet on site as I had planned. Sierra Leone, home of the Mende script, was also torn by war, so I could not visit there either. However, I visited Foumban in Cameroon, where I made wonderful discoveries about the Bamum syllabary, and Calabar in southeastern Nigeria, where I hoped to learn more about Nsibidi, the secret writing of the Ejagham or Ekoi people.

I can safely say that I have traveled widely. But nothing could ever have prepared me for the "high" of meeting the King of the Bamum people, Sultan Ibrahim Mbombo Njoya. I had always heard the claim in the West that the Bamum syllabary was extinct. But one fateful day – October 21, 1997 – I read in the *New York Times* that the grandson of the king who invented the Bamum script a century ago was preserving and promoting Bamum culture by advocating the national adoption of the Bamum syllabary. I clipped the article and carefully stored it in a folder. I made a slide of it and used it in the presentations on Afrikan alphabets that I give at lectures and design conferences around the world. I dreamed of meeting the king in person some day and seeing, first hand, the work of his grandfather. Most books on writing systems gloss over, if they mention at all, the unique achievements of King Ibrahim Njoya who ruled in Foumban from 1886 until 1930. I was surprised to discover that the writing system that he invented, Shü-mom, which is widely referred to as the Bamum syllabary, is alive and well and is taught at the palace. The syllabary was not "extinct." My soul broke into a secret smile as I learned about Njoya's achievements first hand. When in 2003 I finally made my way to Cameroon, I floated around the palace intoxicated by a potent mix of awe and euphoria.

From Foumban I journeyed to Calabar, a city on the Nigerian coast, by way of the capital, Lagos. With a population one-tenth the size of metropolitan Lagos, Calabar offered an antidote to the chaos and frenetic energy of the Nigerian capital, a city whose pulse beats like no other. Today Calabar exports palm oil, but its strategic position on the Gulf of Guinea made it a slave-trading center in the nineteenth century. Having travelled throughout the USA and Cuba previously, with my stop in Calabar I was completing a backward odyssey of the slave trade triangle – first, North America and Europe, where goods from the Caribbean were delivered; then Cuba, where slaves from West Afrika were sold; and now back to Calabar, where Afrikan peoples were captured and taken from the coast of Afrika to the plantations of the Caribbean as slaves.

To get to Havana in 1996 I flew Cubana, the Cuban national airline. The old two-propeller Russian plane felt like an old school bus. Cuba was a strange step into the past. Riding in a Russian Lada (the people's car) into Havana, I thought I had stumbled on a Hollywood movie set about Chicago in the 1940s. Most of the cars were American circa the forties and fifties, each and every one a prized collector's item back in the States. I called it the land of yin and yang – everything stood in stark contrast. There was a sad beauty about the place; magnificent buildings that had seen a better time were crumbling, their original coats of paint peeling and window panes long gone. Decay never looked so beautiful. I say this, of course, at the danger of

Time warp
An immaculate 50s American sedan is parked next to a billboard ringing in the New Year Cuban style. Havana, 1997

romanticizing other people's misery, but I fell in love with the Cuban masses' spirit. Most go to bed hungry, and, although there are more doctors per capita than in the U.S., the U.S.-led embargo deprives the country of medicines.

I felt that Havana had provided the answer for why I came to Cuba: it was there that I ran into (or did it find me?) Anaforuana, the secret writing of the Abakua secret society, which originated in Nigeria. On my second visit in 1997 I attended a Santería ceremony, and when I went to the Santería Museum in Havana a few days later, I marveled that the Cubans had done a better job of preserving their Afrikan past than most Afrikan countries.

La Capitalio, Havana, Cuba
It was in this magnificent building that I first met Alexis Gelabert (see page 8), whose work was on exhibit there.

Crumbling Beauty
The bittersweet beauty of Havana architecture: a block of apartments in Havana Viejo, (Old Havana) along the famed Malacon Avenue.

Afro-Cubano music
I met this group of musicians at a hotel in Havana Viejo in 1997 on my second visit. I loved their music so much they invited me to their rehearsal a few days later. We drank *mojitos* and smoked *Cohibas* and had a grand old time. I spoke no Spanish and they didn't speak any English but we got along just fine!

A painting of Chango given to me as a present by the artist Alexis Gelabert, in Havana, 1997.

The story of Santería itself is an engaging one: Afrikan slaves in Cuba in the nineteenth century would gather on weekends and call upon their Afrikan spirits playing drums. This was a practice that the slave masters found threatening – they thought all this reminder of home might influence them to revolt or run away. They banned these gatherings and imposed the Catholic religion on them instead. The slaves found this Catholic religion boring, so they renamed their Afrikan gods (Orishas) after Catholic saints. For instance, Chango (Shango) the God of Thunder became Saint Barbara, Yemayá (Yemaja) Queen of the Seas became the Virgin Mary; Eleggua (Elegba) who represents good and evil became Saint Anthony. This enabled them to worship their Orishas freely – often winning some of the souls of the masters. In Havana, I found more pride in being Afrikan than I see back home in my own Zimbabwe, where traditional ways have been thrown aside in favor of Western culture. It is widely believed that Afrikan religion (Santería) is the unofficial religion (Catholicism being the official) of Cuba, cutting a wide swath across race and class. Many people go to church on Sunday but consult the Orishas at the altars in their living rooms on a day-to-day basis. This is also true in Haiti, Brazil, and Trinidad where the worship of Orishas was revitalized by exposure to Catholicism and became Voodoo, Candomblé, and Orisha respectively.

Film festival billboard
The logo shown on the billboard is a film camera made up of elements of Abakua signs. See page 113.

18 Festival Internacional del Nuevo Cine LatinoAmericano
3-13 Diciembre-1996 La Habana, Cuba

The artist Alexis Gelabert poses with a portrait of me which he presented as a surprise gift on the eve of my 1997 departure from the island. The painting, done in colored inks and chalk pastels, shows me as an Orisha in a plate of offerings. *"Saki, my hermano, you are my Elegua because you bring me wealth and good fortune. This painting represents the bond between us as brothers and the solidarity between the people of Zimbabwe and Cuba. The Abakua signs speak of that bond. Your hat is the ship that brought us here and dancing on it are our Orishas led by Bob Marley singing songs of freedom!"* Overcome with emotion I wept as I accepted his gift.

While I was researching this book, I was often asked whether I was going to deal with the linguistic characteristics of the writing systems I was working on. Most people would exclaim how "cool" it would be to read the scripts; but since I am not a linguist my response was that it would surely be nice if this could be done. In this book, however, we shall only show the writing systems and, where possible, the basic sounds or meanings of each.

Certain Afrikan peoples have been able to preserve their collective memory through time and transmit it orally from generation to generation. In my view, there is not a single Afrikan society without a system, however rudimentary, to preserve the oral communication of certain messages. The support of this common memory and the material of coded communication are essential for group cohesion, collective identity, and permanence, and for contact with other societies.

Writing preserves a permanent record of the deepest beliefs of a people. Uncovering Afrikan writing systems as I researched this book strengthened my understanding of my continent and my self. The stereotype is that Afrikans have no written tradition. The truth is that Afrikans have known writing since very early in the history of humanity. Some Afrikan nations, some Afrikan ethnic groups, and some individual Afrikan artists endowed themselves with writing very recently. There is appropriate information storage for every group as it develops economically and socially. There is a form of information storage that fulfills its purpose in preserving, sharing, and expressing beliefs for every stage.

So what does all this add up to? Afrikan alphabets reflect the considerable artistic ability and aesthetic sensibility of Afrikan peoples – not just images, but also music and storytelling – throughout the continent. But in their evolution the alphabets also reflect the imprint of history in a wider context: politics, religion, colonization, migration through the slave trade, expatriate influences eventually being imported back into the world in which they started, but subtly changed. Afrikan alphabets are a true reflection of the notion that achievement is shaped by the necessities of the environment of the people who use them.

Roots of Afrikan Writing Systems

frikan alphabets are born out of an oral story-telling tradition and have grown up in a variety of forms across the Afrikan continent and the Diaspora. Some of these communication systems were created several thousand years ago and are inextricably linked to the culture and ideas from which they came. Their purpose has been primarily to preserve a collective memory and, additionally, to create a permanent record.

In this section pictographs and symbols – used in pictographic rock art, scarification, knotted strings, tally sticks, and symbol writing – are considered together as forerunners of writing in Afrika. They form the roots, both directly and indirectly, of Afrikan writing systems.

The commonly held belief is that most graphic symbols in Afrikan societies are merely decorative. In fact, in Afrikan culture, symbols fill an important communication role. There are stories to be found in the rock art of the San people in southern Afrika; the carvings on the calabashes of the Kikuyu of Kenya. There is information stored in tally sticks like the Ishango Bone from The Congo, the knotted strings of Nigerian Aroko, and the scarification found in many Afrikan societies. The meaning attributed to these symbols and artifacts qualifies as proto-writing, or forerunners of writing. Most of these symbol systems are several thousand years old, suggesting that Afrika has a much older tradition of writing than some have recognized.

This chapter on the forerunners of writing systems demonstrates the transition of graphic characters from symbolic reminders to the phonetic codes of spoken language. Tifinagh, for example, once geometric directional symbols painted on rocks to guide nomadic peoples, is today a phonetic alphabet of commerce.

Jokwe pictograph from Angola
The top figure is God, the bottom is Man, on the left is the Sun and on the right is the Moon. The labyrinth-like path starts from and leads to God.

Pictographs

The complex pictograph shown opposite was found among the Jokwe people of Angola. It tells the story of the beginning of the world.

Here is one version of that "story" conveyed using a Western alphabet system and more than 300 words.

Once upon a time the Sun went to pay his respects to God. He walked for many days until he found the path that led to God. Upon presenting himself to God, he was given a cock and instructed to return the next morning before he set off on his long journey back. Sun slept soundly all night and was awakened by the cock, which crowed loudly. He then went to see God, who said, "I heard the cock crow, the one I gave you for supper. You may keep him, but you must return every morning." This is why the sun encircles the earth and appears every morning.

The Moon also went to visit God and was given a cock – who also woke him up in the morning. God said to him, "I see that you also did not eat the cock I gave you for supper. Well done, but come back and see me every twenty-eight days."

Man went to see God too, and was also given a cock. Tired and hungry after his long trip, he ate half the cock and left the rest for his return trip. When he finally woke up, the sun was already high in the sky. He quickly ate the remainder of the cock and hurried to see God. God smiled at him and said, "What about the cock I gave you yesterday? I did not hear him crow this morning."

The man got scared and stammered, "I was hungry . . . and ate him."

"It's all right," said God, "but listen: you know that Sun and Moon have been here, but neither of them killed the cock I gave them. That is why they will never die. You killed yours and so you must die as he did, but at your death you must return here." And so it is.

Barkcloths, painted
Foragers, Ituri Forest
Democratic Republic of Congo
20th century
lengths 23 and 32 inches
(58.4 and 81.2cm)

Bark cloth is made of tree bark that has been pounded flat by the menfolk of foraging peoples from the Ituri Forest in the the northeast of The Congo. (I call it Afrikan paper.) The women use a natural fiber brush to paint the cloth with abstract and rhythmic patterns using an ink made from the juice of the gardenia plant. It is thought that the flowing designs – similar to the motifs painted on their bodies – relate to forest flora and fauna. It is also thought that, in the context of rituals, the designs encode a forest idiom which echoes a unique polyphonic praise sung only by the forest dwellers. Abstractly, it is a form of written communication.

Collection of Dr. Marshall W. and Caroline Mount
The African Art Museum of the SMA Fathers,
Tenafly, NJ
Photo: Tapiwa Muronda

Ntshakishwepi
Embroidered Prestige Wrapper
wood, pigment
161.25 x 72 x 10 inches
(409.6 x 182.9 x 25.4 cm)

Ntshakishwepi (Kuba cloth) are
raffia weavings sewn into a large
wraparound cloth with black
embroidered patterns spaced
irregularly. The individual elements
of the patterns, squares, rectangles,
angles, circles, ellipses – though not
arranged in harmony with each
other, still form a harmonious whole.
Ntshakishwepi are used for daily
wear, but very long examples with
spectacular patterns that "move"
across the length of the fabric are
prestige or dance skirts wrapped
many times around the hips. The
Kuba also make and use raffia skirts
for men.

The African Art Museum of the SMA Fathers,
Tenafly, NJ
Photo: Tapiwa Muronda

15

Symbols

Every culture has symbols. In the United States today, every citizen has a social security number, which gives complete access to all kinds of data on individuals – their mother's name, credit status, etc. This number is far more important than the person's name in establishing who they are. In most countries today, products are imprinted with a bar code, the Universal Product Code symbol, which tells how much a product – whether a sponge or a stove – costs, where, when, and by whom it was made. These twenty-first-century symbols are replacing writing in a digital world, just as writing replaced pictorial symbols in the first two millennia of world civilization. As the world turns digital, as computers take over our lives more and more, writing is converted into code; for example, ASCII – American Standard Code for Information Interchange – a set of numbers used for digital storage and transmission. The spoken word is not exempt from this translation into non-verbal representation: SMS – Short Message Service – sends text messages to and from mobile telephones through the Global System for Mobiles (GSM). With over 600 million GSM users in Afrika, Europe, and Asia, billions of SMS messages are sent worldwide. That figure will grow exponentially once the United States fully adopts GSM in a few years.

The U.S. government developed the internet for military purposes. But those opposed to military conflict are also able to use this technology for peaceful uses that include the transmission of the spoken word (SMS) and the sharing of information (World Wide Web) to spread information globally in ways never thought possible before. And it is not just high technology that is embracing the use of symbols. In public spaces, restrooms are marked with male and female figures; at intersections letters spelling out **WALK** on traffic lights have been replaced with universal ideograms of a human figure frozen in mid-step, and the **DON'T WALK** sign is a red hand held up in a forbidding gesture.

Afrikans utilized symbols rather than words in their personal identification since the dawn of time in body painting and scarification or cicatrisation. Body painting among the Nuba in Sudan has an aesthetic, but it follows precise rules and indicates status. In many societies there are different face painting

Non-representative body and facial design, stamped body design

Face and body painting in Southeastern Nuba, Kordofan province, Sudan, follows precise social rules, and the decorations serve as a status indicator.

Photograph © by James C. Faris from *Nuba Personal Art*. Duckworth, London, 1972

styles and colors for different functions. Similarly, in the Congo societies practice scarification by treating gashes with caustic plant juices to form blisters, which when healed, form raised scars, known as keloids. The shapes and designs can carry permanent symbolism, much as tattoos do in other cultures. Throughout Afrika, personal art serves to mark age, rank, status, or membership in a group.

Reclining (or dead) figure
with an animal mask found at the
Rusape caves.
Rock Art found on walls at
Gwangwadza, Zimbabwe.

The Rock Art of the San People (Hunters and Gatherers) of Southern Afrika

Rock painting abounds throughout the world, from the Lascaux caves of France to the cliffs of Arizona in the United States. In Afrika, rock art is found over the entire continent (see map on page 21). The best-known examples are the rock paintings of South Afrika.

The Khoisan, or San as they are commonly known, were the first inhabitants of southern Afrika, from Zimbabwe to South Afrika by way of Botswana. They are hunters and gatherers who have lived in the area of the Kalahari Desert for thousands of years. They speak the Khoisan language, known for its "clicks." They number only 100,000.

As hunters and gatherers, they have a vast body of knowledge about their environment, especially its plants and herbs. For instance, they have always known of the health benefits of rooibos (red bush), from which a tea that is rich in anti-oxidants and minerals is made. That bush, which grows in the southwestern tip of South Afrika, was their secret until foreigners claimed it. For decades only South Afrikans knew of it until Europe and Japan jumped on the bandwagon. Then the Americans caught on and a woman from Texas patented rooibos tea, (a tea that the San always thought belonged to everyone) locking her and the South Afrikan government and the rooibos tea industry there in fierce litigation for years. Another local plant that the San have used over time to suppress hunger pangs is currently being developed as an anti-obesity drug for use in the West. Under reported terms of the agreement, the San will receive regular fees as the drug goes through the various stages of testing, and they reportedly will also receive a proportion of the royalties.

The San left a huge legacy of rock art in southern Afrika that can be found openly on rocks exposed to the elements. The numerous sites are evidence that Afrikans have co-existed with this art for centuries; in fact, traditionally they have always revered the sites and viewed them as sacred shrines of the spirits. They still use the sites for spiritual purposes. For instance, the site at Domboshava, just outside Harare in Zimbabwe, depicts a rainmaking ceremony, which is common in the area to this day.

The rock art of the San people was originally thought, by European experts, to be a surviving remnant of the original art of ancient Egypt and Crete because its content is so complex. Some experts maintain it is the work of shamans who illustrated their experiences while in a trance. In fact, it is not wise to generalize about San rock art because the work covers not only a large geographical area, but also a huge time span. Some rock art in South Afrika was painted a century ago, while other San paintings in Zimbabwe are thousands of years old.

The stylization of San imagery shows the painters had a strong command of composition. The rock painters depicted types rather than drawing portraits when they showed the men hunting and the women gathering. The images are strictly codified so that the subjects are idealized to represent each person's role in society. The details that would make the paintings look realistic are intentionally omitted. As in other symbolic systems, the individual artist conformed to the style and form of other rock painting. This conformity imposed unvarying rules over all rock painters over thousands of years, hundreds of generations.

Rock art of ancient Afrikans can also be found in the eroded cliffs of Tassili-n-Ajer in Algeria. Long ago, before the Sahara became a desert, this area was home to hunters and gatherers. The animals they hunted do not survive in today's Sahara Desert but can still be found in the savannas of southern Afrika. These paintings – from thousands of years ago – are the proof we have of life as it was lived before the Sahara slowly became a desert.

The Dogon people of Mali still depict great events by painting them on the walls of sacred cliffs. Their drawings on the rocks show stories that adult members of the community intend to pass on to the young. Generation after generation, the Dogon renew the stories that have been on the rocks for hundreds of years, while adding additional designs that tell new stories.

Locations of Rock Art
The shaded areas on this map show locations of rock art. The concentration of rock art on the continent roughly mirrors the points of origin of all Afrikan alphabets.

Detail of art found at Gwangwadza, Zimbabwe.
Top Right
Detail of the art found at Rusape in the eastern part of Zimbabwe.

Photos courtesy of Zimbabwe Museum of Natural Sciences

Right
It is a long steep climb to the top of this rocky hill then a walk halfway down to the Domboshava cave entrance on the other side.

Domboshava (Red Rock) Cave
Above: The art is protected by barbed wire.
Top right: The cave entrance is well hidden from sight by a growth of trees.

Detail of Domboshava art
Middle right: Rhinoceros and antelope
Bottom right: Elephant among other animals found in the art at Domboshava.

23

Nswatubi Cave
In Matobo National Park near Bulawayo, Zimbabwe's second largest city, in the south west.

Mnemonic Devices

Afrikans have always kept records, particularly numerical records – the passage of time, financial transactions, and scores in games. Tally sticks and knotted strings were widely used for this purpose.

Cowrie shells, pebbles, and beans were used for counting and record-keeping across the Afrikan continent. Knotted strings were used to keep track of numerical relationships among the Tshokwe, Bushoong, and Kpelle.

In some Afrikan cultures, a young man has to pay a dowry to his future in-laws before they can permit him to marry their daughter. In the past, those not rich enough could work out installment plans that sometimes spanned a few years. Two strings were used to keep a record of payment, one for the in-laws and the other for the son-in-law. If the dowry was ten head of cattle, ten knots would be made on both strings. A knot was undone every time a payment was made. At the end of his payments, the son-in-law took his string to his in-laws and they compared the two. If both had all knots undone, the debt had been paid in full.

Yoruba messages on a string

The Yoruba of Nigeria developed *Aroko*, a symbolic system using string, cowrie shells and feathers to convey messages. Aroko uses direct symbolism, as in the figure on the right, in which two cowries, back to back, serve as a reprimand from a creditor to a bad debtor ("I shall turn my back on you").

The rebus principle is applied in the second example below. Here six (in Yoruba, *efa*) cowries suggest the word for pull (*fa*). This message says, "By these six cowries I draw you to myself, and you should also draw closely to me." Using this principle in English, one might use the picture of a bee plus a picture of a leaf to convey the word "belief."

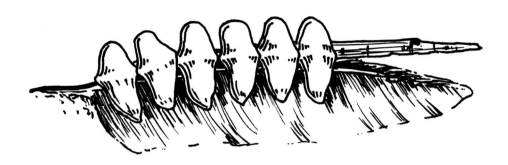

Aroko Message from a prince to his brother living abroad.

Six cowries all turned in the same direction and a bird's feather (used for cleaning one's ears). "Six" = éfà in Yoruba, suggesting the verb "to pull" = fà.

Implied message:

Èfà yi ni mo fi fà mora, ki 'wo na si fà mo mi girigiri.

(By these six cowries I draw you to myself, and you should also draw closely to me.)

Lye yi ni mo fi nreti, ni kankansi ni ki nri o.

(As by this feather I can reach your ears, so I am hoping to see you immediately.)

Ishango Bone: Early Afrikan Mathematics

The use of tally sticks was widespread until the twentieth century. Before colonialization, a pregnant woman in Zimbabwe had the record of her pregnancy kept by her husband, who marked notches on a stick at the beginning of each lunar month. Marks were also made to indicate the time the baby was finally born. The final month of the pregnancy is still known in Zimbabwe as the "month of the staff." Tally sticks had been in use in England by the British Exchequer to record taxes owed and paid from the twelfth century until 1826.

The discovery of the Ishango bone fifty years ago in Ishango, Congo, in the foothills of the mighty Ruwenzori Mountain ranges, near the border with Uganda, gave support to Afrika's long mathematical tradition. The

carved baboon bone (10 cm long or about 4 inches) was a tool handle inscribed on both sides. There are three separate columns, each consisting of sets of notches arranged in distinct patterns. Three notches have been made at the top of the bone, followed by 6, 4, then 8 notches. This suggests that the farmers of this region thousands of years ago knew how to multiply by two. Adding together the number of notches in each column gives totals that are all divisible by twelve, suggesting a tally of lunar periods. This has led some researchers to wonder if the bone was used by women to keep track of their menstrual periods.

The cyclical nature of menstruation has played a major role in the development of counting, mathematics, and the measuring of time. Lunar markings found on prehistoric bone fragments show how early women marked their cycles and thus began to mark time. Women were possibly the first observers of the basic periodicity of nature, the periodicity upon which all later scientific observations were made.

The Akan Symbol Systems

Background

The Akan people – the Asante and the Fante peoples of Ghana and the Baule and the Agni peoples of Côte d'Ivoire – live in the coastal areas of these West Afrikan countries. The Asante state was founded in 1700 by Akan leaders as a confederacy of five smaller states. The Asante confederacy developed into a major trading power, centered inland at Kumasi, controlling the lucrative gold and slave-trading routes to the north and south. A hundred years later, the Asante state had grown into a powerful empire incorporating many non-Akan peoples, ruled by a divine king whose wealthy court made lavish use of gold and gold-plated regalia.

Like other powerful West Afrikan states of the 18th and 19th centuries, the Asante soon threatened European gold and slave-trading facilities along the coast. After a series of clashes with the British, the Asante were defeated, and in 1900 their land became the British colonial possession called the Gold Coast. In 1957 the Gold Coast colony, renamed Ghana, became the first independent Afrikan state and Kwame Nkrumah its first Prime Minister.

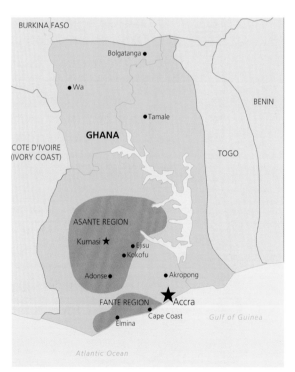

The Akan people: the Asante and the Fante peoples of Ghana and the Baule and the Agni peoples of Côte d'Ivoire.

Akan Gold Weights

Akan weights are a unique phenomenon in Afrika. The weights were cast out of brass, and used by the many Akan and Akan-related peoples between the years 1400 and 1900 for weighing gold

28

dust. As the Akan acquired new trading partners, they added more sizes of weights. Eventually, they had developed sixty different units of weight, of many different figures and abstract geometric designs. The weights were so attractive that they were sought long after their weight values were no longer used in trade.

Akan weights, beyond their practical function, are also recognized as forerunners of writing. Figurative designs came to represent the local wisdom of proverbs or cultural events. They were used as mnemonic devices for these stories and wise sayings, and sometimes sent as three-dimensional messages.

The weights were usually carried in small bags called *adja*, which enabled the owner to tell a story, or remember a commercial transaction, a treaty, or an act of justice. Different bags had different contents. Mixed in the same bag, weights of diverse complexity and significance were sometimes drawn out at random like tarot cards, and then it was up to the storyteller to interpret. Today there is hardly anyone left who can interpret the weights. Some elderly Akan people remember that an image was once associated with a proverb. Out of context, behind glass in museums, each weight is reduced to a semantic unit of a proto-language. But in the glory days of the Asante empire, these weights had the functions of language.

The diversity of the weights in shape and form was immense. There were geometric gold weights, gold weights representing human figures, gold weights representing animals, gold weights representing artifacts, and gold weights cast directly from nature. It was, indeed, a complicated and time-consuming art.

Gold weights representing human figures
Ghana
Brass

Collection of the author
Photos by Tapiwa Muronda

Gold weights representing animals
Ghana, Côte d'Ivoire
Brass

Collection of Helen Ramsaran, New York City
Photos by Tapiwa Muronda

Gold weights representing artifacts
Ghana, Côte d'Ivoire
Brass

Gold weights representing artifacts
Ghana
Brass

Adinkra cloth

Adinkra is the traditional mourning cloth of the Asanti people of Ghana. The cloth at left, commercially woven and dyed, has been cut into six wide strips and assembled to make the wrapper. The patterns are produced with a dye made from tree bark mixed with iron slag by stamping motifs with pieces of calabash carved in relief. A comb-like tool is used to make the linear patterns.

   Mate masie, the circular symbol that runs diagonally across the cloth, implies the message "I understand." It is a symbol of wisdom and knowledge. The meanings and implications of other symbols featured on this cloth can be found on the pages that follow.

Collection of the African Art Museum of the SMA Fathers, Tenafly, New Jersey
Gift of Dr. Pascal James & Eleanor M. Imperato

Photo: Tapiwa Muronda

Akan stools: *Ahema Dwa* and *Kotoko Dwa*

(Queen Mother Stools)
Ghana
Wood
Stools, designed by the Akan peoples, the originators of Adinkra symbols

Courtesy of Hemingway Gallery, New York City

Adinkra Symbols

The Adinkra symbols of the Akan people of Ghana and Côte d'Ivoire are the most widely recognized form of proto-writing in Afrika. These motifs are stylized designs representing proverbs, historical events, and attitudes as well as objects, animals, and plants. They are printed on lengths of cloth that are worn and displayed at important occasions. *Adinkra* means "goodbye" in the Akan language. Originally, the cloths were worn at funerals but today they are displayed at weddings, initiation rites, and naming ceremonies. Blanket-stitched silk and cotton are stamped with a calabash gourd into which Adinkra designs have been cut. The designs are printed in a viscous black ink made from the sap of the badie tree. Once printed, the cloths are never washed because the water-soluble ink will run.

The Adinkra symbol system originated four hundred years ago. Tradition has it that Adinkera was a famous king of the Gyaman (now Côte d'Ivoire). He angered the Twi-speaking Asante king, Nana Osei Bonsu-Panyin, by trying to copy his symbol of Asante power, the Golden Stool. King Bonsu-Panvin killed Adinkera and took his robe as a trophy. Today Adinkra symbols are printed on pottery and metal as well as cloth. They are incorporated into architecture and sculpture.

The motifs of Adinkra symbolism have names and meanings that derive from either a proverb, an historical event, human attitudes, animal and plant life, or the forms and shapes of inanimate and man-made objects. They are very graphic, drawn with stylized geometric shapes. Adinkra symbolism is a visual representation of social thought relating to the history, philosophy, and religious beliefs of the Akan peoples of Ghana and Côte d'Ivoire. The names and meanings of the small selection of symbols shown on the following pages are translated into English from Twi, the language of the Akan peoples.

Sankofa
"Return and get it"
Learn from the past

Adinkrahene
Chief of Adinkra signs
Greatness, charisma,
leadership

Nkyimkyim
"Twistings of life"
Initiative, dynamism,
versatility

Nsa
"Katamanso umbrella –
the covering of the
nation". Protection

Duafe
Wooden comb
Patience, fondness, care

Nkonsonkonson
"Linked together"
Unity, Human relations

Gye Nyame
"I fear none, except God"
Omnipotence of God

Dwanimen
Ram's horns
Strength and humility

Obi nka obie
"Bite not one another"
Symbol of unity,
peace, and harmony

Msusyidie
"That which removes evil"
Sanctity, good fortune

Nsirewa
"Let's live together"
Unity, harmony

Nyame Dua
An altar to the sky God
The presence of God

**Funtunfunefu
Denkyemfunefu**
"Siamese crocodiles"
Democracy, unity in diversity

Papani amma yenju Kramo
"The fake and genuine look alike"
Hypocrisy

Akoma ntoaso
Linked hearts
Understanding,
agreement

Fofoo se die fofoo pe ne se gyinantwi abo bedie
Jealousy

 Ako-Ben
War horn
Call to arms

 Owuo Atweede
"Ladder of death will be climbed by all"
Mortality

 Mpuannum
Five tufts of hair
A traditionally fashionable hair style

 Tabon
Strength and perseverence

 Kuntinkantan
"Puffed up extravagance"
The need for humility

 Sepow
Execution knife used to prevent invoking a curse on the King

 Agyindawuru
Sap of tree used in making gongs whose sound pleases the spirits

 Kuntinkantan
(Same as above)
The need for humility

 Wawa Aba
Wawa is a hard wood used in carving
Strength

 Epa
"You are the slave of him whose handcuffs you wear." Servitude

 Kode Emower Ewa (talons of the eagle)
Loyalty, devotion to service

 Hye wo nhye
Symbol of forgiveness: turn the other cheek

 Nkonsonnkonson
Chain links, a symbol of unity and human relations

 Mmra Krado
Seal of law and order, a symbol of the authority of the court

35

Bantu Symbol Systems

Prehistoric peoples recorded events using very basic symbols to remind them of the past. These pictorial reminders, called pictographs or pictographic writing, developed to the next stage: ideographs. Ideographs are made by simplifying pictographs. A pictograph of a typical man is further streamlined into, perhaps, a vertical ellipse with four appendages. Although it identified a man, it bore none of the details that tell anything about the man. As the symbols became more and more abstract, as the picture component gave way to a pure symbol, the languages had to be taught rather than intuited. That is when humans discovered another great thing about language: it could be used for power and secret knowledge, private messages. At first language was meant to build up communication between people; but then it was used to shut the uninitiated out.

The Bantu symbols give no suggestion of how a word or idea should be pronounced. It is a language to be read silently, not read aloud. Conveying ideas in this silent way takes on a variety of forms. Temporary messages are burned on calabash gourds. Sentiments of love are woven in message mats using beads. Ideas of a more permanent nature, and especially those intended for future generations, are engraved on drums, pottery, and the walls of dwelling places. After a newly-wed couple have built their house, the mother of the husband, or any of his friends, may decorate the house with blessing symbols. This custom is still practiced in Zimbabwe and Mozambique. The Ma-Pochs and Ndebele of South Afrika decorate their dwellings most elaborately with all kinds of prayers, proverbs, and occult sayings.

Credo Mutwa, a Zulu from South Afrika, is the grandson of a medicine man. As an adult, Mutwa underwent the "Ceremony of Purification" in order to begin training as a medicine man. He assumed the post of Custodian of Sacred Tribal Relics upon his grandfather's death. In the course of reclaiming his Afrikan heritage, Mutwa has given much thought to the form in which cultural information is passed along from generation to generation.

Bantu Symbol Systems are used in areas of South Afrika. The Ma-Poch and Ndebele peoples of South Afrika decorate their dwellings most elaborately with all kinds of prayers, proverbs, and occult sayings using the symbols.

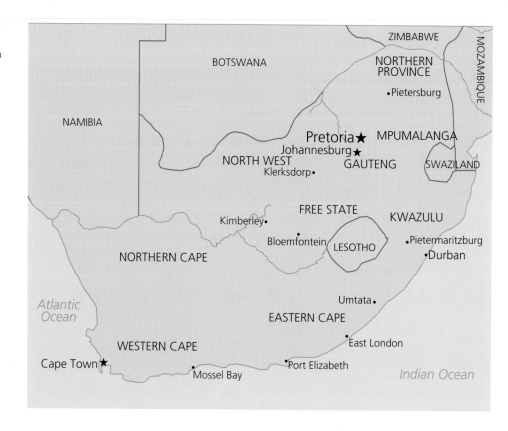

In Afrika, medicine men like Mutwa's ancestors used language both to impart information to a new generation and to keep that same information out of the hands of ordinary people. They created symbols only fellow practitioners understood. In other groups, similar secret languages were used for communication in secret societies; for example, the Ejagham of southern Nigeria and northern Cameroon created Nsibidi for their exclusive use. This was based on social ties rather than a shared body of wisdom.

Bantu Symbol Writing

In South Afrika, the Bantu symbol-language is not taught to the common people. Yet Mutwa estimates thirty percent of the Bantu people could write in this language. Apart from medicine men and the elders and the wise ones, it is mostly women who still employ it. Bantu symbol-language is not a language like Arabic or Swahili. Each symbol does not represent a single character or letter; instead, each expresses a whole word or, more often, a complete idea, much like Chinese and Japanese symbols. The characters are arranged in sequence to communicate a fact: Man+sees+Lion. Lion+eats+ox.

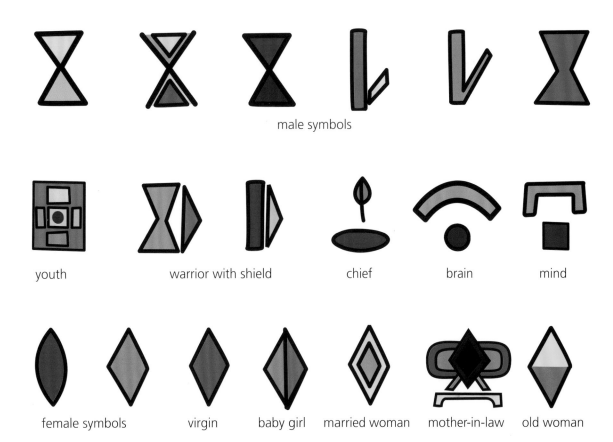

male symbols

youth   warrior with shield   chief   brain   mind

female symbols   virgin   baby girl   married woman   mother-in-law   old woman

bride   beautiful visitor   queen   goddess of creation, mother, source

     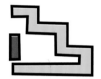

chieftainess   planter, skillful person   vagabond, useless person

marriage, unity, love   birth (figurative and actual)   home

fire, lust, love, passion   unity   break-up, divorce

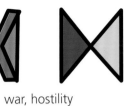 

war, hostility   divine guidance   greatness

sunlight   sunrise, birth   sunset, old age   future

pleasure, joy   obedience   wisdom, silence   conversation

gossip   pollution   madness

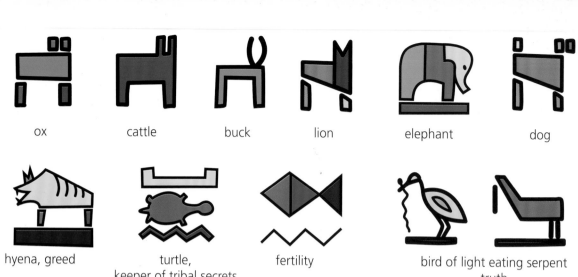

ox cattle buck lion elephant dog

hyena, greed

turtle,
keeper of tribal secrets

fertility

bird of light eating serpent
truth

insect, bee, diligence bird, speed, all haste river, tranquility

   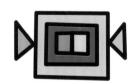

see eat hut home home of in-laws

BY EMMLY MASANABO

Ndebele Painters

In South Afrika, the Ndebele women house painters of *Kwa Ndebele* provinc
have attracted international attention. Esther Mahlangu was commissioned
by BMW to paint an Art Car. She is the first woman artist to be commissionec
by the auto maker to contribute to this series that includes top artists from
around the world. British Airways, in a corporate identity campaign from
1997 to 2000, used designs by twin sisters, Emmly and Martha Masanabo, on

Ndebele planes for British Airways

The women of the Ndebele people replaster the outside of their homes every four years and paint them in bright, bold geometric patterns drawn from the beadwork for which the Ndebele people are known.

Twin sisters, Emmly and Martha Masanabo, two respected house painters from Mpumalanga Province, South Afrika, were commissioned by British Airways to paint panels for the tail fins of 747s as part of a Corporate Identity program during 1997–2000 that included work by many international artists. The tailfin design shown on the 747 above is a detail of the design shown on page 43. The panel (at right) is designed by Martha Masanabo.

Courtesy British Airways Plc, 2003

MARTHA MASANABO

BMW Ndebele Art Car

Since the 1970s the German auto-maker has commissioned artists from around the globe to design a series of Art Cars. In 1991 Esther Mahlangu, a renowned house painter from Mpumalanga Province, South Afrika, became the first woman in BMW's international list of Art Car artists. Her art has evolved from the tradition of home decoration for which the Ndebele people are famous.

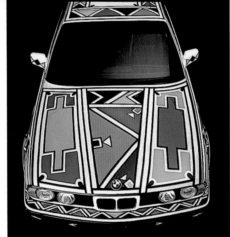

The Alphabet of the Tuareg

Background: the Tuareg

The Tuareg, by tradition, are desert dwellers. Before colonization, they inhabited an area called Tamazgha, which stretched from the Atlantic Ocean on the west to the Red Sea on the east. Over the centuries they have found themselves displaced and separated by the boundaries imposed on Afrika by colonizers.

Today the Tuareg are found in Algeria, Libya, Niger, Mali, and Burkina Faso. The main Tuareg groups are: Ahaggar from Algeria, Ghat from Libya, Air from Niger, Azawagh from Niger-Mali, and Adghagh from Mali. To this day the Tuareg exist in an uneasy alliance with the countries that have swallowed them, and there have been numerous clashes. Reports by human rights groups like the United Nations High Commission for Refugees have shown grave abuses against them. *Berber* is the name that has been given to these heterogeneous nomadic peoples.

Berber merchants have been responsible for bringing goods on camels from the northern end of the Sahara to the great cities of the South. The Berber alphabet existed for 2,000 years and is used to write the languages of northwest Afrika; also Tuareg use it to write their language, Tifinagh. Tifinagh is thought to mean "Punic/Phoenician" in the Berber language. Like other Berber scripts, it has remained largely unchanged over time as a consonant-only alphabet, although vowels have been added recently.

Tifinagh has resisted the influence of foreign systems like the Roman and Arabic alphabets. It is used in coded messages in games, or directions inscribed on rocks as a guide to finding water or game in the desert; and it is also used to pass on secret messages and write private letters.

In January 2003, the Tifinagh alphabet was adopted over the Roman and the Arabic alphabets by the Administrative Council of the Royal Institute for Amazigh Culture to teach Amazigh in Morocco. French designer and typographer Pierre di Sciullo digitized the alphabet, which can be downloaded from his website. This is a major cultural victory for this minority group, which could mean their survival as they become more and more assimilated into the countries surrounding them.

Tifinagh Alphabet

Tifinagh, the modern form of the Berber script, is used by the Tuareg people of Algeria and Libya for writing their Tamasheq language. It has been an alphabet of consonants only, with vowels sounds a recent addition. It is written without spaces between the words. It has a geometric style that makes it convenient for inscriptions on rock or tracing on the palm of a conspiring hand.

The Tifinagh alphabet

•	a	⟐	b	+	t
:	u	◺	b̲ (v)	×	t̲
÷	é	⊐	f	⊨	ts
Σ	i	ꓘ	k	Ƴ	ṭ
∪	w	⤶	ḳ	∧	d
∩	y	‖	l	∨	d̲
Φ	h	|	n	E	ḍ
⋏	h	ⵝ	ḡ	Ω	ḍ
⌢	eh	ⵥ	g	ơ	s
Ɀ	q	ⵤ	dj	O	r
Ⴗ	ġ (gh)	Ɪ	j	⊙	s
✗	(kh)	Ϲ	ch	✗	z
⊏	m	Ꙅ	tch	✹	ż

The usual posture taken by Tuareg writers of Tifinagh as they draw messages in the sand.

The text below was written by Aboubacar Allal, a Tuareg silversmith from Niger I met in New York. The Tifinagh characters differ from region to region – each group has slightly different characters.

∴ Ⅰ∴ ɵ:ɵ∴ O ·ǀǀ·ǀǀ ⟨Ⅰ·⊏·#ǀǀ Υ∴⟨ǀǀ

ⴲꙅO∴Ⅰ ··O⟨E∶ ·⊏⟨Oⵒ∶· ⴲ⟨ǀǀ

⫟ꙅE⟨ǀǀꙅ⫟ Υ ⫟∴OⱵ⟨ Υⵛⵛⵛ⊏·#ꙅ∴⊦

(It is me, Aboubacar Allal, artist from the Kel Ferouaue (Tuareg Group). I have come to America to look for customers for Tuareg crafts.)

48

Historical Afrikan Writing Systems

The **Afrikan alphabets** characterized as historic range widely in their dates of origin. Some date from thousands of years ago (Ethiopic), some are hundreds of years ago (Nsibidi), some are from the early 20th century (Shü-mom and Vai), and some date from the comparatively recent times of the mid-20th century (Mende, Loma, and Kpelle).

The desire to express ideas and relay and record information – selectively, but for posterity – is an ancient concept. While many of the new alphabets are based on what has gone before, many individuals and Afrikan societies have felt the need for their own means of expression. What sets these writing systems apart from other Afrikan writing systems is that they continue to be in use today – some by millions of people – in all the written communication of their daily lives. There continues to be an interest in the teaching of these Afrikan alphabets to both the young and other initiates in order to preserve and continue cultural traditions.

Ethiopic ፊደል

It is popularly thought that Ethiopic has Semitic origins, developing from the script of Ethiopia's classical language, Ge'ez, which was derived from the Sabaean/Minean script brought to Eritrea from south Arabia over 2,500 years ago. The script used to write Ge'ez has been in use since at least the 4th century AD. At first the script represented only consonants; vowel indication was added in around 350 AD, when the 22 consonants took on vowel indications for the 7 vowel sounds of the Ge'ez language. They were written with small appendages to the consonant letters, with modifications of their shapes.

In contrast to popular thought, the Ethiopian semioticist, Ayele Bekerie, maintains that the Ethiopic writing system is, from the beginning, the work of an Afrikan people and can be defined as a system of knowledge through concretized symbols because it incorporates philosophical features. His book *Ethiopic, An African Writing System* is a comprehensive study of this writing system, defining it as a writing system that expresses the Ethiopian cultural identity and their sense of connectedness to the people of the world.

51

Ge'ez Bible

Above: A manuscript Bible featuring Ge'ez, an Ethiopic script.
Right: Rubrication and decorative elements of this book dating from the 19th century.

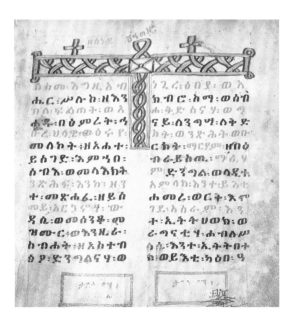

Ethiopic Script

Ethiopic script in its classic state has a total of 182 syllographs, which are arranged in seven columns, each column containing 26 syllographs.

Each symbol represents a syllable consisting of a consonant plus a vowel. The basic signs are modified in a number of different ways to indicate the various vowels.

Written horizontally from left to right, words in inscriptions are separated with a vertical line. Elsewhere, two dots similar to a colon are used to separate words, although in languages such as Amharic, blank spaces are generally used instead. A full stop or period is four dots (::) and a comma is two dots with horizontal lines over and between them.

This script is used to write Amharic, the national language of Ethiopia, which has about 14 million speakers.

The Ethiopic Writing System

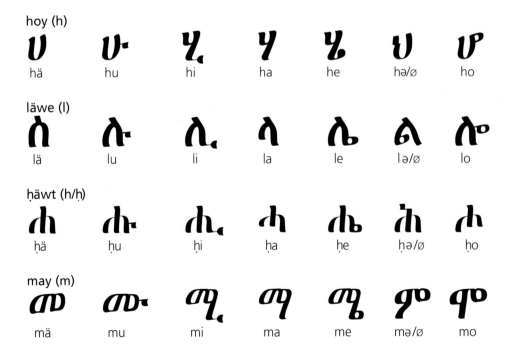

hoy (h)

hä   hu   hi   ha   he   hə/ø   ho

läwe (l)

lä   lu   li   la   le   lə/ø   lo

ḥäwt (h/ḥ)

ḥä   ḥu   ḥi   ḥa   ḥe   ḥə/ø   ḥo

may (m)

mä   mu   mi   ma   me   mə/ø   mo

53

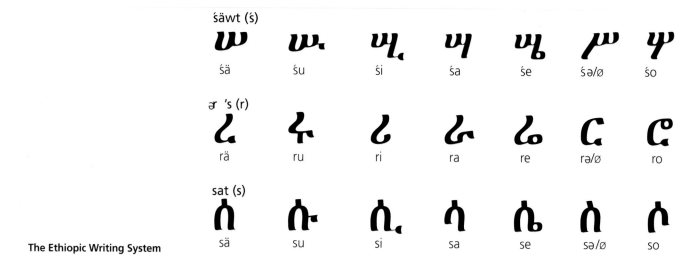

śäwt (ś)

śä	śu	śi	śa	śe	śə/ø	śo

ᒋ ′s (r)

rä	ru	ri	ra	re	rə/ø	ro

sat (s)

sä	su	si	sa	se	sə/ø	so

The Ethiopic Writing System

Vowel sounds
ä = open a as in "art"
long **u** = "ooo" as in "use"
long **i** = i as "lie"
long and short **a** = "play" & "cat"
long and short **e** = "feet" & "fret"
ə (schwah) = indeterminate "eh/ah" sound of unstressed syllables
long and short **o** = "toe" & "tot"

The Ethiopic Writing System

š

sä	su	si	sa	se	sə/ø	so

qaf (q)

qä	qu	qi	qa	qe	qə/ø	qo

qaf (q)

quä		qui	qua	que	quə

bet (b)

bä	bu	bi	ba	be	bə/ø	bo

täwe (t)

tä	tu	ti	ta	te	tə/ø	to

č

čä	ču	či	ča	če	čə/ø	čo

ḫärm (h/h)

ḫä	ḫu	ḫi	ḫa	ḫe	ḫə/ø	ḫo

55

härm (h/h)

᎑		᎒	᎓	᎔	᎕
ẖuä		ẖui	ẖua	ẖue	ẖuə

nähas (n)

ነ	ኑ	ኒ	ና	ኔ	ን	ኖ
nä	nu	ni	na	ne	nə/ø	no

ñ

ኘ	ኙ	ኚ	ኛ	ኜ	ኝ	ኞ
ñä	ñu	ñi	ña	ñe	ñə/ø	ño

The Ethiopic Writing System

'älf

አ	ኡ	ኢ	አ	ኤ	እ	ኦ
'ä	'u	'i	'a	'e	ə/ø	'o

kaf (k)

ከ	ኩ	ኪ	ካ	ኬ	ክ	ኮ
kä	ku	ki	ka	ke	kə/ø	ko

kaf (k)

ኰ		ኲ	ኳ	ኴ	ኵ
kuä		kui	kua	kue	kuə

h

ኸ	ኹ	ኺ	ኻ	ኼ	ኽ	ኾ
hä	hu	hi	ha	he	hə/ø	ho

wäwe (w)

ወ	ዉ	ዊ	ዋ	ዌ	ው	ዎ
wä	wu	wi	wa	we	wə/ø	wo

'äyn

ዐ	ዑ	ዒ	ዓ	ዔ	ዕ	ዖ
'ä	'u	'i	'a	'e	'ə/ø	o

zäy (z)

ዘ	ዙ	ዚ	ዛ	ዜ	ዝ	ዞ
za	zu	zi	za	ze	zə/ø	zo

ž

ዠ	ዡ	ዢ	ዣ	ዤ	ዥ	ዦ
žä	žu	ži	ža	že	žə/ø	žo

yämän (y)

የ	ዩ	ዪ	ያ	ዬ	ይ	ዮ
yä	yu	yi	ya	ye	yə/ø	yo

dänt (d)

ደ	ዱ	ዲ	ዳ	ዴ	ድ	ዶ
dä	du	di	da	de	də/ø	do

ğ

ጀ	ጁ	ጂ	ጃ	ጄ	ጅ	ጆ
ğä	ğu	ği	ğa	ğe	ğə/ø	ğo

gäml (g)

ገ	ጉ	ጊ	ጋ	ጌ	ግ	ጎ
gä	gu	gi	ga	ge	gə/ø	go

gäml

ጐ		ጒ	ጓ	ጔ	ጕ
guä		gui	gua	gue	guə

ṭyät

ጠ	ጡ	ጢ	ጣ	ጤ	ጥ	ጦ
ṭä	ṭu	ṭi	ṭa	ṭe	ṭə/ø	ṭo

č

ጨ	ጩ	ጪ	ጫ	ጬ	ጭ	ጮ
čä	ču	či	ča	če	čə/ø	čo

ṗäyt

ጰ	ጱ	ጲ	ጳ	ጴ	ጵ	ጶ
ṗä	ṗu	ṗi	ṗa	ṗe	ṗə/ø	ṗo

sädäy

ጸ	ጹ	ጺ	ጻ	ጼ	ጽ	ጾ
ṣä	ṣu	ṣi	ṣa	ṣe	ṣə/ø	ṣo

däṗṗa (s/z)

ፀ	ፁ	ፂ	ፃ	ፄ	ፅ	ፆ
ẓä	ẓu	ẓi	ẓa	ẓe	ẓə/ø	ẓo

The Ethiopic Writing System

äf (f)

fä	fu	fi	fa	fe	fə/ø	fo

psa (p)

pä	pu	pi	pa	pe	pə/ø	po

The Ethiopic Writing System

Ethiopic numbers:

1	2	3	4	5	6	7	8	9
10	20	30	40	50	60	70	80	90
100	1000							

Ethiopic consonants:

h	l	h	m	s	r	s	s	q	qu	b
t	c	k	h	w		z	z	y	d	g
g	gu	t	c							

59

Talismanic characters

Gera, 1992
ink on paper
19.75 x 27.5 inches (50 x 70 cm)
Private collection

Gera, the artist who created the talismanic characters on the right, is a traditional scholar of the Ethiopian Orthodox Church. Known for his skill in esoteric arts, he was asked to teach his art to the public. He came to identify himself as an artist and produced these characters for a show in Paris.

Ethiopian scholars see the origins of all writing in symbols like these that resemble letters of the Ethiopic syllabary. Talismanic properties are those that possess occult powers or offer protection from evil.

Photograph courtesy Jacques Mercier.

Poet's Journal (opposite page)

Wosene Kosrof, 2002
acrylic on canvas
17.5 x 18 inches (44.5 x 45.5 cm)

In the words of the artist: "This painting portrays the mind of a poet: the word play that a poet experiences, the search for meaning and metaphor. It breaks apart words and glues them back together in a continually new visual expression. As part of my series *The Color of Words*, 'Poet's Journal' is about how language is itself an expression of the human condition; it's not about words and their meanings, but rather my work is about language as visual form and color."

Courtesy of Mulatu Kosrof,
Addis Ababa, Ethiopia
Photographed by Black Cat Studio, San Rafael, CA

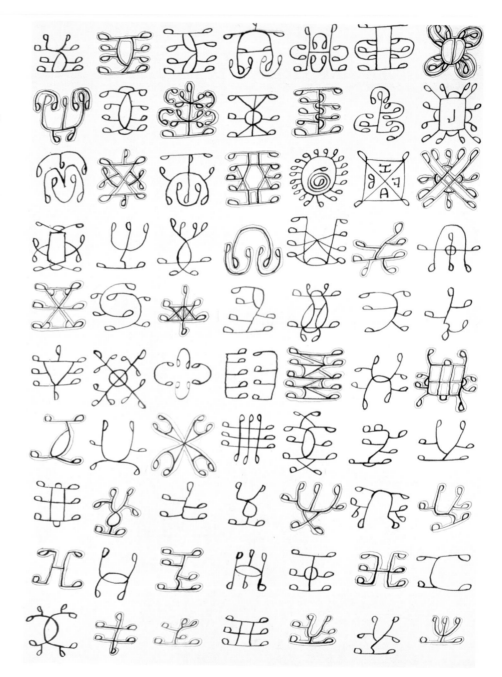

The Mande Syllabaries

Researching West Afrikan writing systems was a challenge. My planned visit to Liberia and Sierra Leone was cancelled because of civil war. I had to rely on secondary sources. The group of indigenous scripts found in Liberia, Sierra Leone and further up north in Mali are called the Mande Syllabaries. Books on the syllabaries were inconsistent in dates and the spelling of names. There are five syllabaries: the Vai, the Loma, and the Kpelle from Liberia; the Mende from Sierra Leone; and the Bambara from northern Mali.

A clear familial relationship exists between the five scripts in the Mande system. They are all syllabaries where each character represents a consonant + vowel. Except for Kpelle, all have similar graphic forms – some sharing identical forms for similar sounds. Except for Mende, all are written from the left to the right. Mende is written right-to-left. Personal correspondence and personal recordkeeping are the primary uses of these scripts. Graphically they were inspired in part by traditional symbols and in part by the secret scripts used to transcribe Arabic in the Hodh region of Mauritania during the period 1830 to 1930.

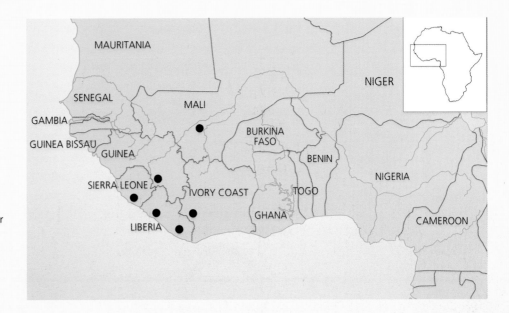

The origins of the five Mande syllabaries are to be found in West Afrika. Their use is not exclusive to defined geographical areas, but rather each one is used in various parts of the region. The countries (indicated by the black circles) where Mande syllabaries are found are Guinea, Côte d'Ivoire (Ivory Coast), Liberia, and Mali.

Dan masks
Wood, Liberia
The Dan, who live in the same areas where the Vai Syllabary is used, are as well known as for their masks as the Vai are for their writing.

The Vai People and their writing system

Of the five syllabaries in the Mande System, the most famous is the Vai. Upon its "discovery" by Europeans in the early 1800s Vai was regarded as an advanced script. The script was taught in numerous schools built over Vai territory and generated a level of popular literacy rare among agrarian societies in any part of the world. The rapid spread of the script served important societal needs since the Vai people in the nineteenth century were vigorous traders. As middlemen between Dutch and Portuguese merchants and the people of the interior, they traded gold, exotic woods, and ivory for salt, tobacco, and metals. A writing system, known only to their people, gave the Vai a large advantage over their Liberian competitors.

The Vai coast had also gained notoriety as a haunt of slavers. By 1807, negotiations required for the procurement, containment, and exchange of large numbers of slaves were complicated because slaving was officially against the law. The British Royal Navy patrolled the Vai coast to suppress the trade, but it thrived well into the middle of the century. The Vai writing system made record keeping and the transmission of messages easier, since negotiations in writing did not require the actual presence of the negotiating parties. Trading in ivory and tobacco is made somewhat more efficient when supported by a written record; illegal trading in slaves is made much more efficient when supported by a "coded" written record. When freed slaves from the United States began to buy land and settle in Vai country, the Vai language gave the indigenous Vai people a way of keeping their community affairs private. Since the newcomers from America did not know the language, they were not able to influence the Vai politically.

Sylvia Scribner and Michael Cole studied the Vai in the 1970s, and state in *The Psychology of Literacy* that literacy among the Vai of Cope Mount in the nineteenth century was greater than literacy in many areas of Europe and the United States during the same period. Unfortunately, whatever had been gained by the Vai in the past has been rendered moot by the devastating civil war that has ravaged Liberia and Sierra Leone for most of the past decade, destroying a way of life known for centuries.

The Vai Syllabary

Edwin Norris, a British naval officer fresh from duty in Liberia, first brought the Vai syllabary to Europe's attention at a lecture to the Royal Geographical Society in 1849. Then in 1854, the German philologist S. W. Koelle researched the Vai language at Cape Mount. He identified Dualu Bukele, a Liberian, as the inventor of the script around the year 1820 when the script was shown to him in a vision. ". . .I had a dream in which a tall, venerable-looking white man, in a long coat, appeared to me saying, 'I am sent to you by other white men . . . I bring you a book.'" The messenger showed Bukele many signs, but he could not remember all of them on waking, so he gathered some friends and together they made new signs.

There are other theories concerning the development of the Vai alphabet. In rural areas, some Vai elders talk of the development of the script from ancient pictographs. Travelers in the region mention the widespread use of graphic symbols in rituals long before Bukele's time. Modern Afrikan scholars give Dualu Bukele credit for phoneticizing the ancient pictographs and creating an efficient syllabary. They do not accept the white-man-in-a-long-coat dream theory.

Today there are approximately 105,000 Vai living in Liberia and Sierra Leone. They are strong advocates of Islam and have built mosques throughout their area.

Vai, the oldest of the Mande syllabaries, is the only script to be used in translations from the Koran and the Bible. The 192 characters are phonetic – they represent the consonant + vowel units language. Vai reads left to right.

The Vai Syllabary

pe	pi	pa	po	pu	poh	peh
be	bi	ba	bo	bu	boh	beh
bhe	bhi	bha	bho	bhu	bhoh	bheh
mbhe	mbhi	mbha	mbho	mbhu	mbhoh	mbheh
kpe	kpi	kpa	kpo	kpu	kpoh	kpeh
mgbe		mgba	mgbo		mgboh	mgbeh
gbe	gbi	gba	gbo	gbu	gboh	gbeh
fe	fi	fa	fo	fu	foh	feh
ve	vi	va	vo	vu	voh	veh

The Vai Syllabary

te	ti	ta	to	tu	toh	teh
de	di	da	do	du	doh	deh
le	li	la	lo	lu	loh	leh
dhe	dhi	dha	dho	dhu	dhoh	dheh
ndhe	ndhi	ndha	ndho	ndhu	ndhoh	ndheh
se	si	sa	so	su	soh	seh
ze	zi	za	zo	zu	zoh	zeh
ce	ci	ca	co	cu	coh	ceh
je	ji	ja	jo	ju	joh	jeh

The Vai Syllabary

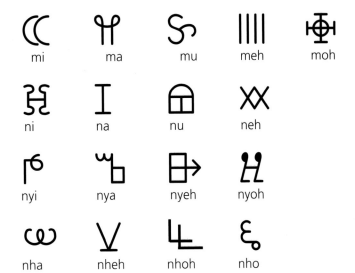

mi	ma	mu	meh	moh
ni	na	nu	neh	
nyi	nya	nyeh	nyoh	
nha	nheh	nhoh	nho	

The Vai Syllabary

The Mende Syllabary (Ki Ka Ku)

The Mende syllabary of Sierra Leone was invented in 1921 by Kisimi Kamara, a Muslim tailor of Portu. It is widely believed that he accomplished the task in thr and a half months. Some of the syllabary characters look like Vai characters, bu Mende, unlike Vai, reads right to left. The syllabary is purely phonetic, without any pictographic origins. It has a total of 195 characters, of which 167 are show below, omitting alternate variations of characters. Mende is used for correspon dence and record keeping, especially accounting.

ku   ka   ki

Mende is read right-to-left. Below and to the right the characters and their sounds have been set left-to-right for easier reading.

ki   ka   ku

pi	pa	pu	pe	peh	pah	po
wi	wa	wu	we	weh	wah	wo
mbi	mba	mbu	mbe	mbeh	mbah	mbo
bi	ba	bu	be	beh	bah	bo
kpi	kpa	kpu	kpe	kpeh	kpah	kpo
gbi	gba	gbu	gbe	gbeh	gbah	gbo

The Mende Syllabary

fi	fa	fu	fe	feh	fah	fo
vi	va	vu	ve	veh	vah	vo
ti	ta	tu	te	teh	tah	to
li	la	lu	le	leh	lah	lo
ndi	nda	ndu	nde	ndeh	ndah	ndo
di	da	du	de		dah	do
si	sa	su	se	seh	sah	so
ji	ja	ju	je	jeh	jah	jo

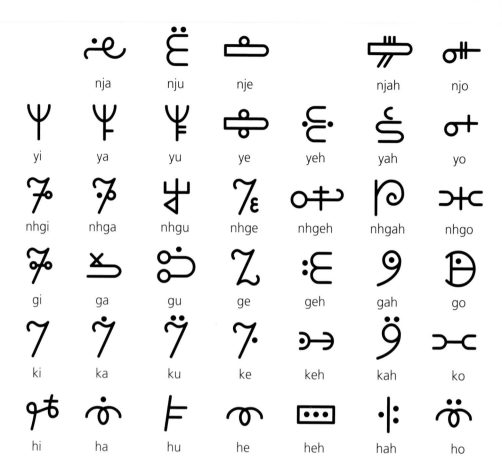

The Mende Syllabary

	nja	nju	nje		njah	njo
yi	ya	yu	ye	yeh	yah	yo
nhgi	nhga	nhgu	nhge	nhgeh	nhgah	nhgo
gi	ga	gu	ge	geh	gah	go
ki	ka	ku	ke	keh	kah	ko
hi	ha	hu	he	heh	hah	ho

Additional syllables

hgua	gua	kua

Nasal syllables

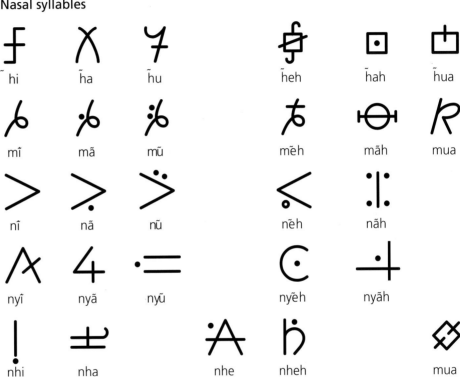

The Mende Syllabary

˜hi	h̃a	h̃u	h̃eh	h̃ah	h̃ua
mĩ	mã	mũ	mẽh	mãh	mua
nĩ	nã	nũ	nẽh	nãh	
nyĩ	nyã	nyũ	nyẽh	nyãh	
nhi	nha	nhe	nheh		mua

The Bambara Syllabary (Ma Sa Ba)

Although belonging to the Mande group of languages (common to both Liberia and Sierra Leone), the Bambara syllabary originated in Mali, near the border with Mauritania in northern Afrika. Woyo Couloubayi, of the Kaarta region, is credited with its invention in 1930. Bambara is spoken by almost 3 million people in Burkina Faso, Côte d'Ivoire, The Gambia, Guinea, Mali, Mauritania and Senegal. It is sometimes written using the N'Ko alphabet. Bambara has 123 letters and is read left to right, like Vai.

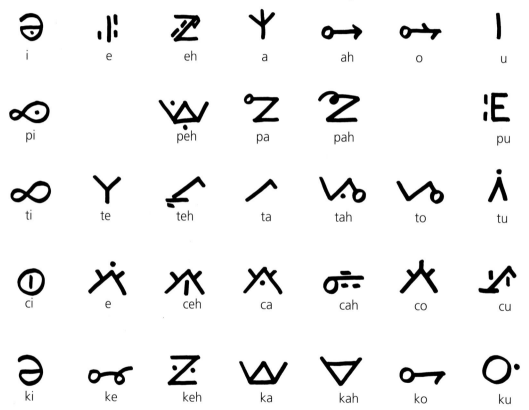

bi	be	beh	ba	bah		bu
di	de	deh	da	dah	do	du
ji	je	jeh	ja	jah	jo	ju
gi	ge	geh	ga	gah	go	gu
fi	fe	feh	fa	fah	fo	fu
si	se	seh	sa	sah	so	su
		nx(z)eh	nx(z)a			
mi		meh	ma	mah		mu

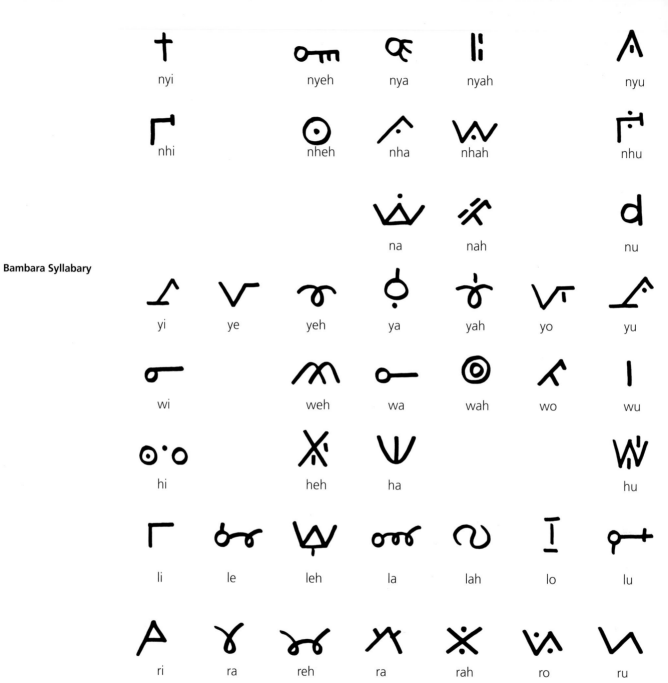

Bambara Syllabary

nyi   nyeh   nya   nyah   nyu

nhi   nheh   nha   nhah   nhu

na   nah   nu

yi   ye   yeh   ya   yah   yo   yu

wi   weh   wa   wah   wo   wu

hi   heh   ha   hu

li   le   leh   la   lah   lo   lu

ri   ra   reh   ra   rah   ro   ru

The Loma Syllabary

Wido Zobo is credited with inventing the Loma syllabary in the 1930s in Liberia. Read left to right, like the Vai but unlike the Mende, it is otherwise similar to the other syllabaries in the Mande family of writing systems.

Loma Syllabary

pi	pa	pu	pe	peh	pah	po
wi	wa		we	weh	wah	wo
bi	ba	bu	be	beh	bah	bo
bhi	bha	bhu	bhe	bheh	bhah	bho
gbi	gba		gbe	gbeh	gbah	gbo
fi	fa	fu	fe		fah	fo
vi	va		ve	veh	vah	vo

The Loma Syllabary

ti	ta	tu	te	teh	tah	to
li	la	lu	le	leh	lah	lo
di	da	du	de	deh	dah	do
si	sa	su	se	seh	sah	so
zi	za	zu	ze	zeh	zah	zo
yi	ya	yu	ye	yeh	yah	yo
ki	ka	ku	ke	keh	kah	ko

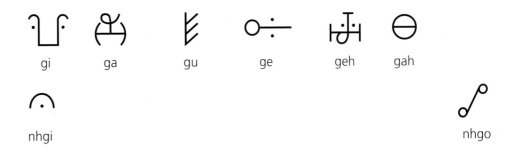

| gi | ga | gu | ge | geh | gah |

| nhgi | | | | | nhgo |

Nasal syllables

The Loma Syllabary

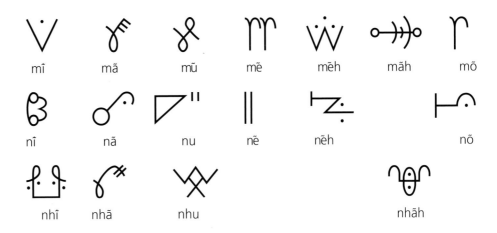

| mĩ | mã | mũ | mẽ | mẽh | mãh | mõ |

| nĩ | nã | nu | nẽ | nẽh | | nõ |

| nhĩ | nhã | nhu | | | nhãh |

The Kpelle Syllabary

The Kpelle syllabary was invented during the 1930s by Chief Gbili of Sanoyea, Liberia. It was used to some extent by speakers of Kpelle in Liberia and Guinea during the 1930s and early 1940s but never achieved popular acceptance. Today Kpelle is usually written with a version of the Latin alphabet.

The Kpelle syllabary consists of graphemes and is written from left to right in horizontal rows. Many of the symbols have more than one form.

This syllabary is used to write Kpelle, a member of Mande group of Niger-Congo languages spoken by about 490,000 people in Liberia and around 300,000 people in Guinea.

Kpelle Syllabary

The Kpelle Syllabary

h(s)i/j(z)i   h(s)a/j(z)a   h(s)u/j(z)u   h(s)e/k(z)e   h(s)eh/j(z)eh   h(s)ah/j(z)ah   h(s)o/j(z)o

ya/nya   yu/nyu   yeh/nyeh   yah/nyah

ki/gi   ka/ga   ku/gu   ke/ge   keh/geh   kah/gah   ko/go

kwi /gwi   kwe/gwe   kweh/gweh

ngi   nga   ngeh

ngwe   ngwah   ngwo

wi/nwi   wa/nwa   wu/nwu   weh/nweh   wah/nwah

Nasal Syllables

mi   ma   mu   mah

nĩ   nã   nũ   nẽ

81

King Njoya's Syllabary

In the year 1896, during the period that Cameroon was colonized by Germany, King Ibrahim Njoya of the Bamum Kingdom undertook a massive effort to develop a system of writing. King Njoya not only invented a writing system at the age of 25, he also left behind a huge collection of his manuscripts detailing the history of his people. He compiled a pharmacopœia, designed a calendar, drew maps of his kingdom, kept administrative records and legal codes, and wrote a Kama Sutra-like book – all this in the Shü-mom writing which he had invented. King Njoya also produced a large collection of drawings. This collection is still housed in the museum that he developed to preserve his people's heritage.

He created this legacy for his people by putting together a group of dignitaries from among his people who were chosen for their intellect and drawing talents. With the notables, especially his cousin Ibrahim Njoya, who was a talented and prolific artist, the king was able to build a large collection of art and records. As a student of Afrikan alphabets and history, I wanted to find out more about this Renaissance man.

Not long after he had built a magnificent palace and built schools for his people, the French took control of Cameroon. Their power was threatened by his achievements. They destroyed the printing press that he invented, destroyed his libraries, and burned many of the books he had written. The French soldiers threw Bamum sacred objects into the street. And finally, in 1931, they sent him into exile in the capital of Yaoundé where he died a broken man in 1933. Over the years, Njoya's son and his heir Seidou Njimoluh quietly worked to preserve his heritage.

After Cameroon claimed its independence from the French in 1960, King Njimoluh collected those objects that had not been destroyed and put them in his father's museum where they could be kept safe. King Njimoluh ruled from 1933 to 1992. Today King Njimoluh's son, Sultan El Hadj Ibrahim Mbombo Njoya, no longer has the political power the dynasty had before the Europeans arrived. However, he continues to keep a watchful eye over the Bamum legacy. I hoped to meet him and discuss his grandfather's work with him.

King Ibrahim Njoya
The 17th king of the Bamum. A Renaissance man whose achievements were destroyed by colonialism, in particular the French.

18 Bamum kings surrounding King Ibrahim Njoya
Ibrahim Njoya, 1938–1940.
Pencil, color pencils, and gouache on paper

Portrait of King Njoya
Ibrahim Njoya, 1920.
Pencil, ink, color pencils on paper
34.5 x 36.5 inches (87.5 x 93 cm)

King Ibrahim Njoya carefully picked the best from among his "notables" to help him devise his writing system. They were all highly talented artists. Among them was his cousin, a very talented draughtsman and painter, who created a prolific body of work. Some of these magnificent drawings are shown on these pages.

Courtesy of Bamum Palace Museum

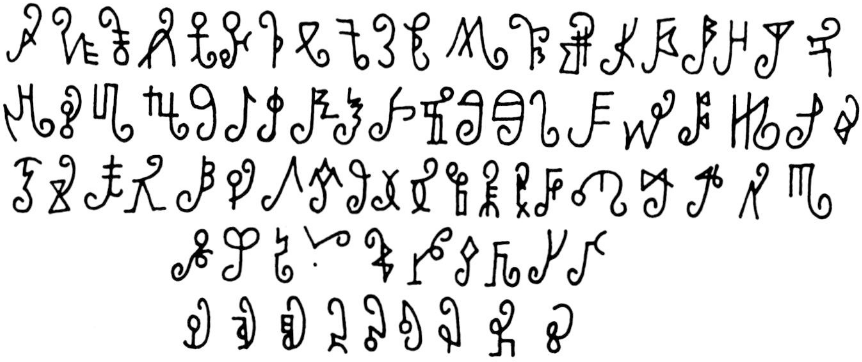

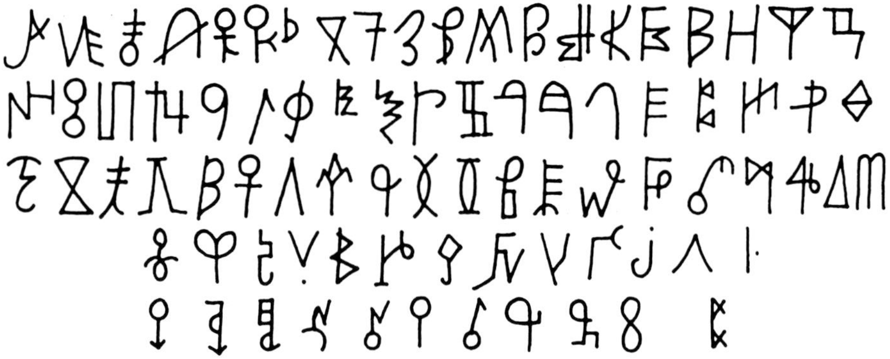

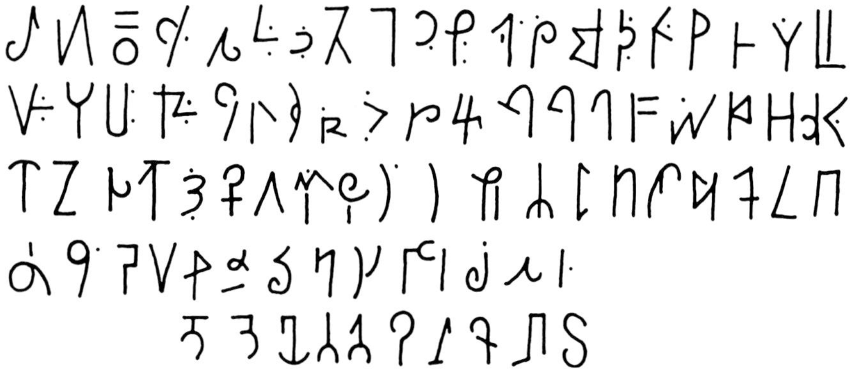

Shü-mom, King Njoya's writing system invented in 1896. Three versions of six developed over 30 years.

Lerawa niet (top)
A Ka u Ku, (middle) and
A Ka u Ku Mfemfe (bottom)
The three versions of Shü-mom show its transition from an elaborate to more simplified cursive script.

a	ka	u	ku	é	Re	te
O	nyi	i	la	Pa	Ri	rié
lé	mé	ta	da	njem	M	Su
Mu	Shi	Si	Shù	sù	Ké	Két
Noue	Nou	Njoue	Yo	Shou	You	Ya
Sha	Kú	pou	jé	té	Pü	Wi
Pé	fé	Rou	Lou	Mi	Ni	Rú
Re	Kén	Kwen	Ga	gna	Cho	Poue
Fou	Fem	Wa	Na	Li	Pi	Lo
Ke	Mbèn	Rèn	Mèn	Ma	Ti	Ki

a   u   e   o   i

The Current Shü-mom Syllabary

King Njoya of the Bamum in Cameroon ruled from 1880 to 1931. After much consideration he decided to create a script for his own people. This first script was logographic, containing 465 signs. Njoya modified his script several times during his reign, each time with fewer and fewer signs, as it slowly morphed into a syllabary using the rebus principle. The final script had just 83 signs: 10 numbers and 73 syllables. Each syllable could have a tone indicator if necessary.

87

Shü-mom Syllabary

Da	Di	Do	Dé
Tou	Dou	tu	
Si	Sé	Sü	
Fou	Vou	Fo	
F,V	Vi	Vé	Fü
Poue	Bo	Bou	Po
Re	Ra	Ro	Rü
Shi	Ji	Shé	Shü
Ke	Ko	Go	Gué	Gi
You	To	Ja	Jou	

The combinations on this page are made in order to write some phonemes that are difficult to make from the 70 characters of the alphabet shown on the previous page.

88

Shü-mom Syllabary

Above text written, in Shü-mom, translates into English as:

Pupil

I am a pupil, my teacher is called Kputayoum, our headmaster is called Ngoupayou. His head is small, he walks like a sheep. Each time that he comes to school, he takes his stick and pupils cry. Each time he departs from school, pupils address insults to him.

My teacher Kputayoum is a good teacher, but my headmaster Ngoupayou is a crook. Pupils have given him a nickname. His nickname is Mister Stick.

89

The first version of Shü-mom.
Ibrahim Njoya, 1897
Pencil on paper
4.75 x 7.5 inches (12 x 19 cm)

Courtesy of Bamum Palace Museum

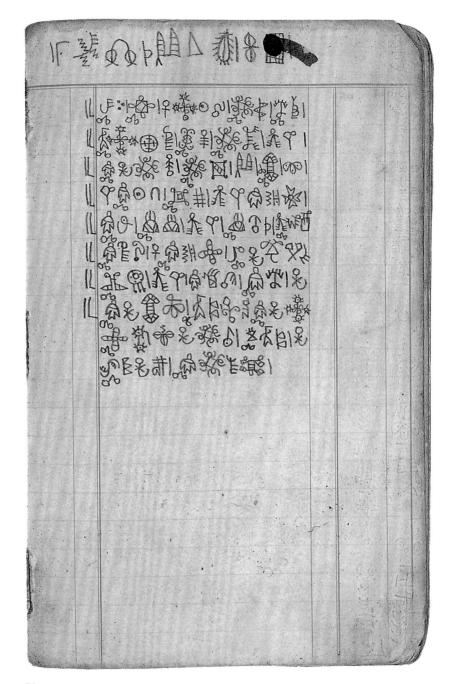

A Page of Shü-mom.
Ibrahim Njoya
Pencil on paper
4.75 x 7.5 inches (12 x 19 cm)

Courtesy of Bamum Palace Museum

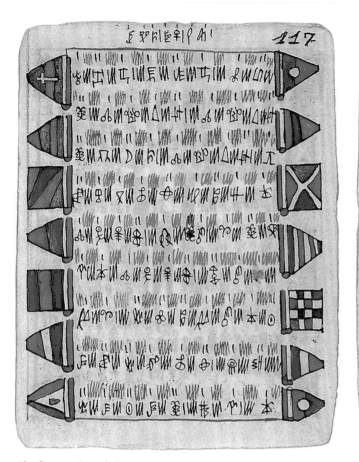

The first version of Shü-mom.
Ibrahim Njoya, 1897
Pencil on paper

Courtesy of Bamum Palace Museum

Calendar in Shü-mom
Ibrahim Njoya, 1897
Pencil on paper

Courtesy of Bamum Palace Museum

93

The Palace façade.
Foumban, Cameroon

Deep in Bamum country

I decided to travel to Cameroon so that I could meet history face-to-face. I was helped by Cameroonian friends in New York who set me up with family contacts. I finally landed in the coastal city of Douala in January 2003. Tucked on the coast and oppressively hot, this bustling city is the commercial capital of Cameroon. I was very well received by my New York friend's family and the next day flew on to Yaoundé, the administrative capital.

I made contact with two professors at Yaoundé University who gave me much information about the king and the palace. Then I took a four-hour ride in a cramped minivan to Foumban, where the king's legendary grandfather had left an incredible alphabetic legacy. The road was very good, and it meandered through lush green countryside with rolling hills in the distance. Cameroon is endowed with an undulating landscape, many small hills, and some mountain ranges. What should have been a four-hour trip, however, took six because of numerous stops by policemen manning countless impromptu roadblocks solely for the purpose of extorting money from the drivers. I arrived in Foumban late in the afternoon, completely wiped out.

Founded in 1394, this capital of the former Bamum empire is a dust bowl in the dry months (when I went) and a mud bath in the rainy season – a condition I could certainly envision, given the thinness of the soil, which rises easily, coating everything with its fine yellow dust as cars zoom past at speeds far too fast for the narrow roads. Although there are minivans ferrying people from one point to another, rattling yellow taxis zip up and down competing for fares, radios blaring local bikutsi music.

The Bamum people had been keeping the artifacts of each monarch in a room under lock and key; King Ibrahim Njoya decided to put them on display for the enjoyment of his subjects. That is how the idea of a museum was born. As a result, there are some magnificent items on display, a few of them dating back to the 14th century.

I find it hard to explain my feelings as I walked through the huge arched entrance to the palace. I stopped a few yards inside the courtyard and let my eyes take in the imposing three-story red brick structure – which is both the King's living quarters and a museum. It was envisioned in 1904 after King

On the way to Foumban
The minivan and the typical landscape we drove through.

95

Njoya visited the German governor's mansion in the coastal town of Buea and decided he could build a better structure befitting a king! European in style, Njoya's palace maintains a uniquely Afrikan sensibility with features like the wooden shutters carved in the signature Bamum style. Life at the palace seemed to go on in a placid but controlled manner. There are all kinds of officials making sure the place runs efficiently. Visitors are encouraged to tour the museum.

The museum occupies the three main floors of the building, with the King's living quarters occupying a smaller section of the grand building, which has about a hundred rooms in all. The collection, huge and impressive in scope – 8,000 manuscripts – had me transfixed. I was mostly interested in Njoya's manuscripts, feasting my eyes upon the genius of this Afrikan son. I looked up at the huge portrait of him at one end of the hall and bowed my head in silent homage. I also found it hard to comprehend why and how this gem of a building and Njoya's legacy have remained unknown, for the most part, not only to the rest of the world but also to us Afrikans.

There's always room for one more package! Transportation Afrikan style at the Foumban market.

Islam is another legacy of the king's grandfather. Raised an animist in the 19th century, King Ibrahim Njoya became a Moslem after observing victorious Arab warriors from the north. He watched them credit their victories to small books of Islamic verses that they kept in little purses sewn into the fronts of their tunics. Soon after the arrival of Europeans, he observed how they obliterated their Arab adversaries with their guns, and when he asked them what their secret was, they pointed to the Bible. Njoya decided the new book was more powerful than the small book of verses, so he adopted Christianity. But he was traditionally a polygamist, and the Europeans told him that he had to give up all his other wives and remain with only one – a proposition he found offensive. So he decided to go back to Islam, since they allowed polygamy. Ultimately he mixed some of his people's animist beliefs with Islam to create a Bamum brand of worship. This explains the drums and fanfare as they go to the mosque.

Every Friday at noon the current king, Sultan el Hadj Ibrahim Mbombo Njoya, goes to pray at the mosque, about 200 yards across the street from the palace. He is surrounded by a slow-moving procession of court musicians clad in bright-colored garments blowing on long brass instruments, drummers beating out intricate rhythms, and singing, ululating women who seem to be trying to outdo each other. The sultan, serene and majestic in flowing robes, smiles as he walks at a crawl in the middle of the crowd, a huge umbrella hoisted over his head to shelter him from the sun. The prayer is short, and soon the procession snakes its way back to the palace.

The sultan makes his way back to the Palace from worship at the mosque. The crowd is made up of his attendants, local townsfolk, and curious tourists and visitors. The sultan is under the huge umbrella.

I met Sultan el Hadj Ibrahim Mbombo Njoya one evening just before sundown. He came out (amidst the music of the court musicians, with visitors and attendants bowing and paying respect) and he stood on the steps of the palace looking regal in his sumptuous robes. Oumarou Nchare, the Director of Cultural Affairs at the Bamum Palace, kept telling me to get ready to meet the king but someone else always beat him for the king's attention. The expectation was killing me. I felt the wetness in my armpits, but my face did not give away my emotions. Finally, Oumarou grabbed my arm and thrust me in front of Sultan Njoya and introduced me to him. Protocol be damned, I was all adrenaline as I held my hand out and he took it in a firm grip as he welcomed me in very good English. He told me he had visited South Afrika, met Mandela, and would love to visit Zimbabwe some day. He asked me how Mugabe was doing. I later learned that prior to inheriting the throne in 1992, he had been a government minister and diplomat for decades; this explained his worldly demeanor. Yet something about him made me very comfortable – he had no airs, one felt that he had a strong connection to the people. A people's king.

Opposite page
Sultan el Hadj Ibrahim Mbombo Njoya, the current and 19th king of the Bamum, beats on a double gong.

Photo courtesy of Palais des Rois Bamoun

Court musicians (top) clad in royal colors jamming on shrilly brass-sounding instruments and large drums that spat out ancient rhythms that spoke of the history of the dynasty.

Visitors bow (bottom) as they greet the king.

In an artisans' village a mile or so from the palace, a community of artists and dealers sells masks and other crafts from west and central Afrika. Since Cameroon is the bridge between these parts of Afrika, there are artists and dealers with beautiful pieces from Congo, Sierra Leone and Equatorial Guinea. The main attraction is the Bamum and Bamileke masks of Cameroon. Elegant in shape and color, these masks are unique to Cameroon and bear no resemblance to anything from any other part of Afrika. Some of the kiosks are run by young teenage boys whose tenacity in making a sale is both admirable and sometimes annoying. They speak both English and French and are determined not to let any customer leave without buying.

Bamum wooden panel (top) carved with the symbols of the Bamum kingdom like the double-headed snake, the double gong, the elephant and the bull.

Collection of Michelle Esso

An artist (at left) adds the finishing touches to a Bamum drum at the artisan village.

Masks (facing page) from Cameroon and other parts of west and central Afrika, on sale at the artisans' village.

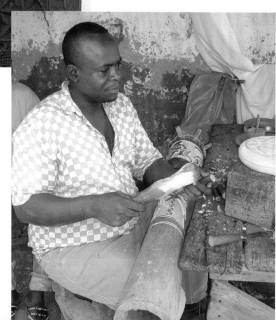

My trip to Calabar, Nigeria, in search of Nsibidi

I journeyed to Calabar, by way of Lagos, right after my trip to Cameroon in early 2003. I came to Calabar in eastern Nigeria with hopes of learning more about Nsibidi, the secret writing of the Ekpe Society of the Efik and the Ejagham peoples.

I visited the Calabar Museum, which houses the relics from the town's long history of slavery. Calabar was a huge slave port, with as many as sixty ships in the harbor at any given point during its heyday. Original letters exchanged by some of the local chiefs and the monarchy in England discussing their trade in human beings are on display in the museum. Some of these chiefs sent their children to be educated by the English, which explains in part the English names that some Calabar families have today.

Evidence of some Afrikans' implicit involvement in slavery was everywhere. This was the first time I had ever been face-to-face with this, and it was difficult to look at a major site of one of the worst cases of human displacement in history. Besides, the obscene profits that the European nations garnered from the slave trade by far eclipse the paltry rewards paid to the Afrikans.

I felt a strange sickness crawl over me as I stood on the banks of the Calabar River, watching boats ferry people back and forth and fishermen in dugout canoes bringing in the catch of the day. I tried to listen to the waters of that mighty river; what sad secrets did she hold deep in her womb? I refocused my eyes after I imagined the sixty or more ships docked at this very spot, all a hive of activity as the crack of the whip echoed over and over late into the night.

The afternoon I arrived in Calabar, I took a stroll downtown. ("Don't stray too far from the hotel, Sir," I was warned by the receptionist at the Mirage Hotel.) I settled in a small bar by the side of a busy road about half a mile from the hotel. It was excruciatingly hot and humid, and every pore of my body was gasping for the relief only an ice-cold beer can provide, so I ordered first a Star Lager then a Gulder, both in quick succession. I sat back in my chair and surveyed the easy flow of traffic controlled by a policeman at

The Badagry Slave Market, near Lagos, Nigeria, one of the first on the Afrikan West Coast, has been well preserved and is an important stop on the tour of slave sites around the town.

From this spot on the Calabar River (opposite page) millions upon millions of Afrikans left the continent for unknown destinations across the oceans. Today motorized boats criss-cross the dark waters ferrying passengers as fishermen paddle their dugouts in search of fish.

the intersection. A smile crossed my lips as I thought that such a scene could never be witnessed in Lagos, with its insane traffic!

Calabar turned out to be the antidote for Lagos's frenetic energy. I turned to the two women who sold cold drinks and hot pepe (pepper) soup. I asked them what they thought of the Efik and their secret religion; they both answered quickly, as if on cue: "They are very, very bad." "How so?" I inquired. "They are not Christians, and they practice pagan worship." Their negative judgment seemed to be based on the fact that the Ekpe religion is animist, a belief that all objects have consciousness and personality.

The Ekpe Tradition and Nsibidi

The Calabar museum displayed a few examples of Nsibidi writing of the Ekpe secret societies, but the veil of secrecy still keeps visitors from finding out everything about this language. The exhibit acknowledged a special secret writing – symbols representing concepts, spread from the Cross River area among the Ejagham (Ekoi) and Efik, a language called Nsibidi. It is important to note that there are other groups in the Cross River area that use the Nsibidi writing system, such as the Ibibio and the Igbo peoples.

The Ekpe secret societies are based on Ekpe, a mysterious spirit who lives in the forest and is supposed to preside at the ceremonies of the Society. Only males can join, boys being initiated about the age of puberty. Members are bound by oath of secrecy, and fees, on entrance, are payable. The Ekpe men are ranked in seven or nine grades, for promotion to each of which fresh initiation ceremonies, fees and oaths are necessary. The Society combines a kind of freemasonry with political and law enforcing aims. For instance, any member wronged in an Ekpe district, an area dominated by the Society, has only to address an Ekpe man or beat the Ekpe drum in the Ekpe house. To "blow Ekpe" as it is called means to sound the Ekpe horn before the hut of the wrongdoer. When this happens the whole machinery of the Society is put in force to see justice done.

Thirst quenchers
Calabar Palm wine, Gulder and Star Lager – Nigeria's most popular lagers.

What is truly remarkable about the Nsibidi alphabet is that each Ekpe lodge in Calabar and its environs has its own collation of symbols that combine with or replace older ones. The Nsibidi alphabet is therefore open. Some symbols are left behind, while others, either new or modified from the old, are created to accommodate contemporary expressions. The only permanence is the script itself. A comparison of all the Nsibidi alphabets in use suggests that there are about 600 signs common to all Ekpe lodges.

Nsibidi

Nsibidi is the ancient writing created by the Ejagham people in southern Nigeria and in the contiguous area of northwestern Cameroon. The Nsibidi language was developed before the 18th century for use by the male Secret Society of the Ekpe (Ekbo), or Leopard Society, in Nigeria. Each Ekpe Secret Society has a visible emblem, a dyed cloth called a *ukara,* bearing signs in the Nsibidi script. The Efik people use the ukara to create a barrier, figurative and real, between initiates and the people, to enhance the Efik collective identity, and to ritualize authority. The presence of the ukara cloth for over two centuries, and over eleven centuries of Nsibidi writing in the Efik cultural landscape, are longstanding and far-reaching social facts. They allow us to appreciate how an Afrikan culture endowed with writing experienced the impact of Western colonization and survived after independence. Nsibidi is still in use today and it is still secret; as a result, researching Nsibidi script turned out to be as elusive and mysterious as the writing system itself.

In his book *Flash of the Spirit,* Robert Farris Thompson describes three levels or types of Nsibidi. First are the common signs that are not secret or mystical. They are the signs even the uninitiated know that represent human relationships and communication.

From the Benin region of Nigeria come magnificent bronzes. Above is a copy of one of the world-famous Benin bronze heads. At right, below is a close-up of a bronze leopard head.

Courtesy the Hemingway Gallery, NYC
Photos Tapiwa Muronda

Second are "dark signs" because they are frequently drawn with solid black areas (see the third row of signs on page 107). They represent danger and extreme distress. Black and white are colors used to represent death and freshness respectively. The third and final group are the secret Nsibidi signs, known only by priests and initiates. They are the important signs of rank and ritual within the Society. These are the signs that would be on the ceremonial ukara cloth.

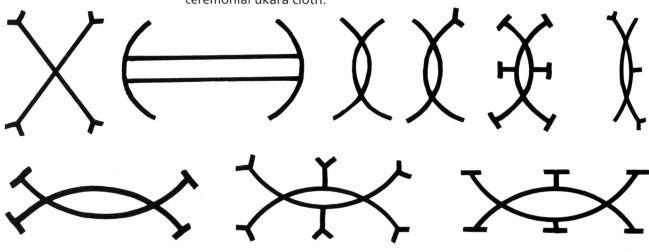

Two rows above:

love, unity and compatibility

Two rows at right:

hatred, disunity, and divorce

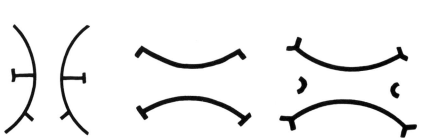

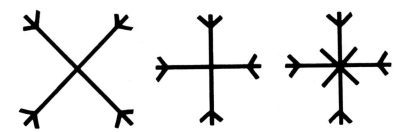

trouble or speech at the crossroads

compatibility

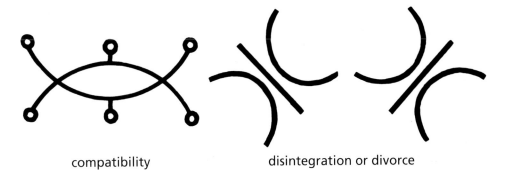

disintegration or divorce

executioner's mirror   killer's sword   dead body

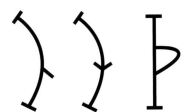

man, woman, pregnant woman

words, speech, meeting or congress

trek, journey, voyaging

feathered sign of membership in the Leopard Society

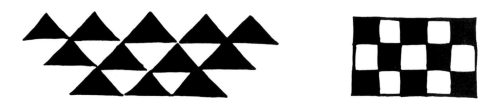

arrangements of triangles and squares stand for the leopard's spots, a sign of leadership and prowess in war

tracks along a path as in the path of love

motion or movement as in dancing

These signs were incised on calabashes by women of the Ibibio, signifying love and praise for their men

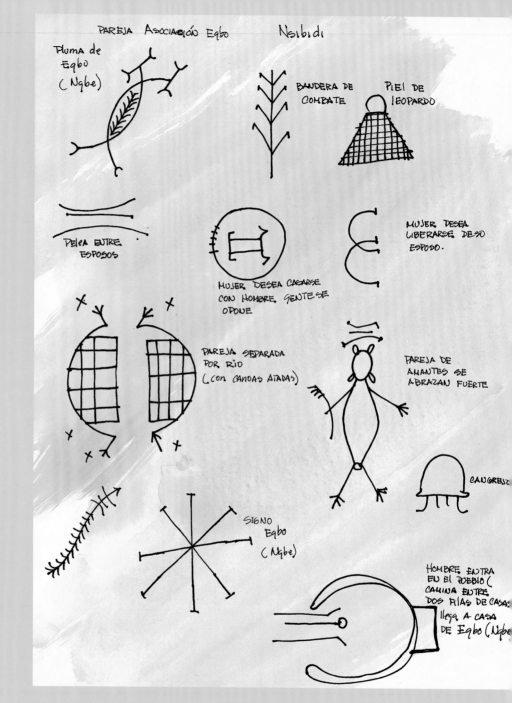

Nsibidi in the New World

Symbols drawn for me by the Cuban Abakua artist, Alexis Gelabert, in Havana. They show that Nsibidi did not change that much in its new location.

Victor Ekpuk, a Nigerian artist, uses Nsibidi in his work.

"These are works from the *manuscript series*. This series is realized in acrylic with found objects on Islamic prayer boards, also called *walaha*. Muslim clerics in Nigeria use these carved wood boards to write prayers or to teach children to write in Arabic scripts.

"When I started exploring the use of ancient writing systems as a means of contemporary visual expression, the idea of the boards as media for literacy in Africa appealed to me. I was fascinated by their shapes as unique sculpture pieces and by their function as bearers of sacred texts.

"The paintings I execute on walaha do not make statements about Islam; rather they are an attempt to forge an intercultural marriage of form and script. Instead of Arabic scripts, I employ Nsibidi signs and my own invented scripts to make compositions with themes that center mostly on the human conditions of joy, pain, and hope.

"The goal of bringing these two disparate cultural and religious symbols together in my work is to create personal and contemporary sacred objects that convey the sacredness and awe that both the walaha and Nsibidi signs inspire."

–*Victor Ekpuk*

© Victor Ekpuk

© Victor Ekpuk

Images courtesy of the artist.

Soothsayer's Mirror
Acrylic on koranic board, 1997
11" x 20" (27.9 x 50.8 cm)

Song of the Cowherd
Acrylic on koranic board, 2000
12" x 23" (30.5 x 58.4 cm)

© Victor Ekpuk

111

Systems of the Afrikan Diaspora

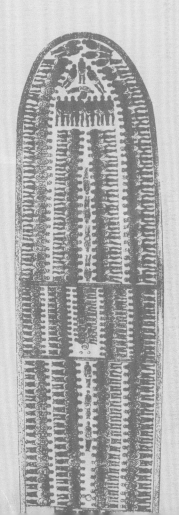

The Afrikan Diaspora, a horrific scattering of enslaved peoples from their homelands to the West, also scattered the languages and writing systems of Afrika to the Caribbean and South America. Whether it be Anaforuana in Cuba, the Djuka syllabary in Suriname on the northeast coast of South America, or Bassa in the jungles of Brazil, alphabets brought from Afrikan societies evolved to meet the need of new environments. These needs included religious and cultural preservation and confidential communication.

A cross-fertilization of the lost cultures and the new cultures resulted. In some cases the new writing system is similar to that left behind – the characters of Anaforuana are similar to those of Nsibidi. In the case of Djuka the characters used for the writing of this language are a blend of remembered Afrikan symbols and those of the Latin and Arabic alphabets. In the case of Vah, the writing system of the Bassa peoples, a writing system that was lost to Afrikans during colonialization was restored from the New World. Vah was found to be actively used among Brazilians and Caribbeans of Bassa origin. It was restored to Liberia in 1900, and continues to be taught in the schools and used for the publication of some Liberian newspapers and literature.

Anaforuana

The slaves from Calabar and Congo took their secret religions with them to the New World. The Ekpe religion, through the persistence of the Nsibidi script invented by the Ejagham people of southeastern Nigeria and northwestern Cameroon, has survived in Cuba. There Ekpe became Abakua and Nsibidi became Anaforuana, the writing of the Abakua secret society. In the following pages I share with you a few of the symbols from a purely aesthetic point of view; all from a book of Anaforuana designs given to me as a gift by the artist, Alexis Gelabert of Havana, Cuba.

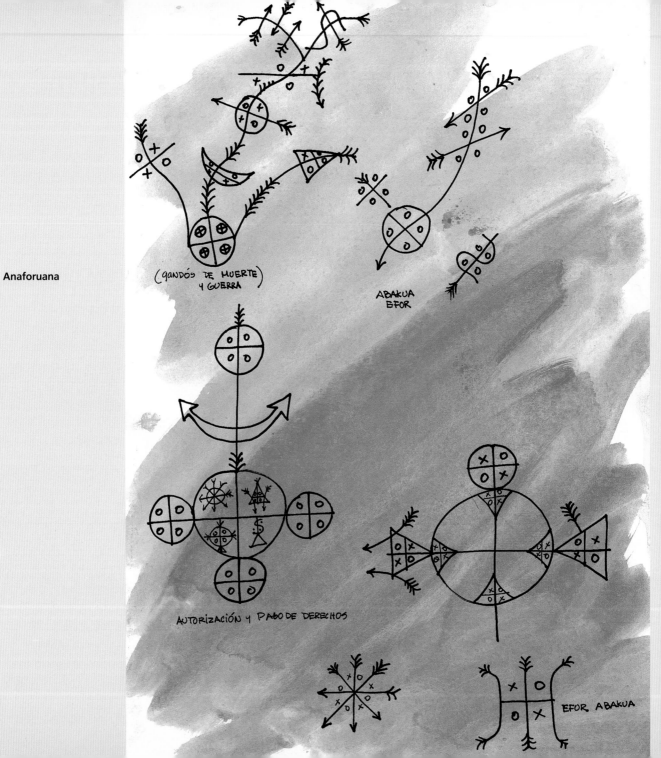

Anaforuana

(gandós de muerte y guerra)

ABAKUA
EFOR

AUTORIZACIÓN Y PAGO DE DERECHOS

EFOR ABAKUA

Anaforuana

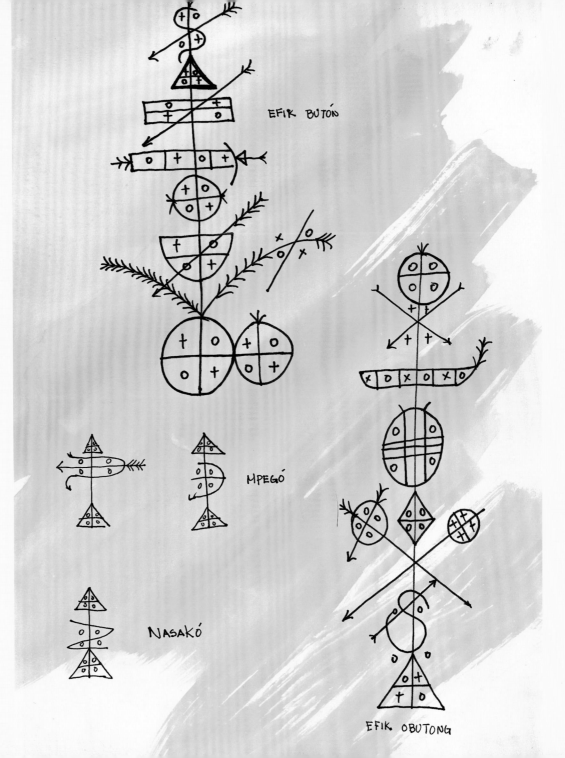

EFIK BUTÓN

MPEGÓ

NASAKÓ

EFIK OBUTONG

Anaforuana

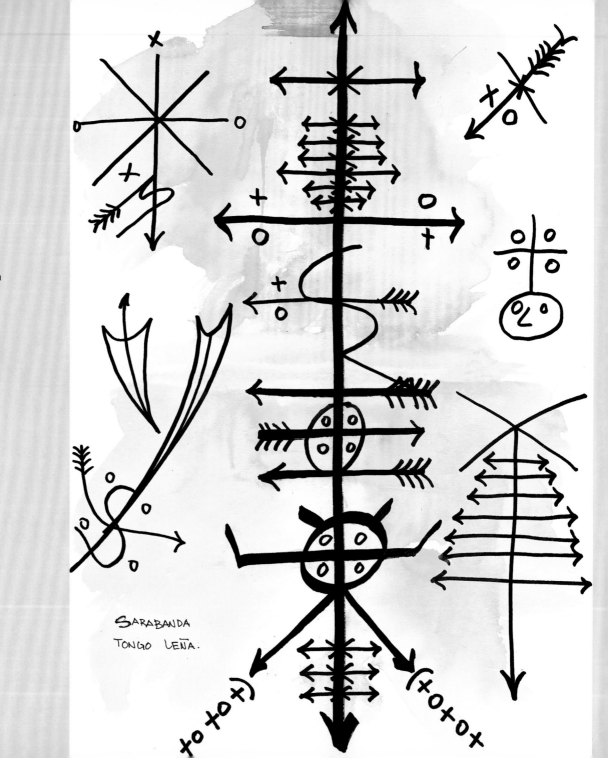

SARABANDA
TONGO LEÑA.

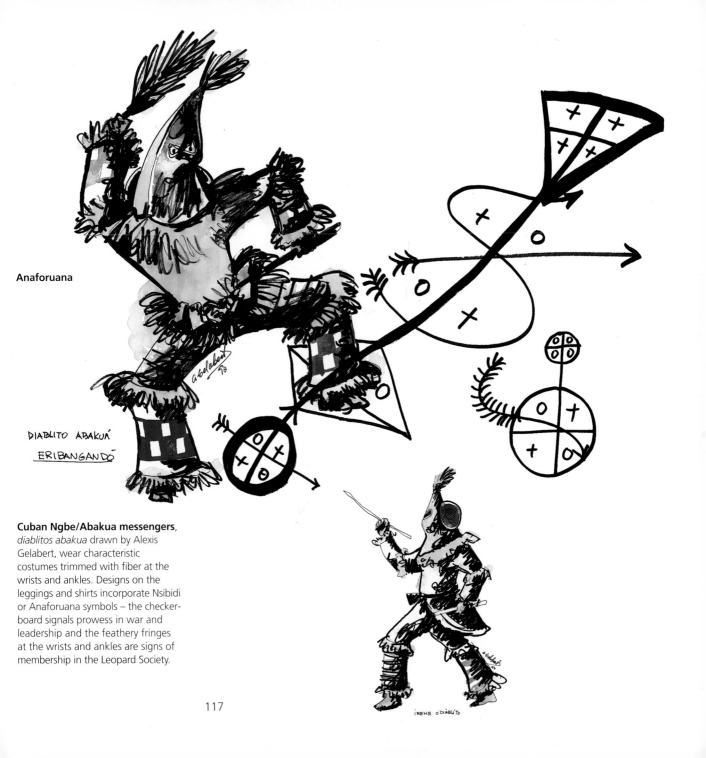

Anaforuana

DIABLITO ABAKUÁ
ERIBANGANDO

Cuban Ngbe/Abakua messengers,
diablitos abakua drawn by Alexis
Gelabert, wear characteristic
costumes trimmed with fiber at the
wrists and ankles. Designs on the
leggings and shirts incorporate Nsibidi
or Anaforuana symbols – the checker-
board signals prowess in war and
leadership and the feathery fringes
at the wrists and ankles are signs of
membership in the Leopard Society.

IREME O DIABLITO

117

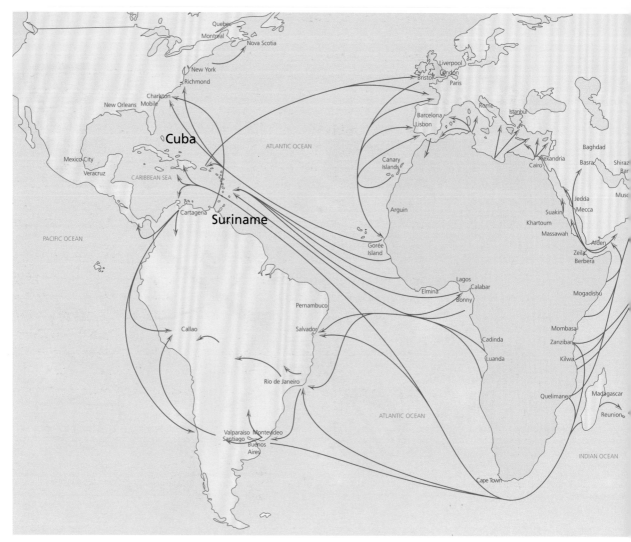

Map showing the infamous slave routes
on which Afrikans were forcibly carried
to unknown destinations.

The Djuka Syllabary of Suriname

The slave trade plucked millions of Afrikans from their homes and carried them to the New World in one of the single largest displacements of humanity in the history of mankind. Not all captives ended up as slaves though; more than a million are estimated to have died during the Atlantic crossing by jumping overboard or succumbing to the inhuman overcrowding and starvation in the ship's holds, where they were packed like sardines. Some, like the Djuka, ran away to freedom once they arrived in the New World. The Djuka ended up deep in the forest in Suriname, on the northeast coast of South America. The Djuka established a homeland rich in Afrikan traditions and culture, and devised a language that is a patois of English, Dutch, and Afrikan languages.

In the early 20th century the Djuka devised their own writing system, a syllabary not unlike its West Afrikan counterparts, the Bamum and Mande syllabaries, which were being developed simultaneously. All drew from a tradition of West Afrikan pictograms and ideograms. Just before the appearance of Halley's Comet in 1910 – in a famous case of synchronicity – a Djuka named Afaka Atumisi had a dream in which a spirit prophesied that a script would be revealed to him. He subsequently devised a series of syllabic characters for writing the Djuka language. Below is the word *Djuka* and Atumisi's pictogram of the comet.

Dju   ka

The sign of Halley's Comet as recorded by Afaka Atumisi, (see page 122).

The Djuka Syllabary

The Djuka syllabary was invented by Afaka Atumisi of eastern Suriname in 1910. The symbols of this syllabary are based on traditional graphic symbols but influenced by Latin and Arabic letters and numbers. It is used to write Ndjuka or Aukaans, English-based Creole spoken by about 25,000 people in Suriname and French Guiana.

Djuka syllabary

a	e	i	o	u
ba	be	bi	bo/bu	
da	de	di	do/du	
fa	fe	fi	fo/fu	
ga	ge	gi	go/gu	
ja	je	ji	djo/dju	

Djuka syllabary

ka ke ki ko/ku kwa

la le/li lo/lu

ma me/mi mo/mu

na ne ni no/nu nja

pa pe pi po pu

sa se/si so/su

ta te ti to tu tja

wa we/wi

121

Djuka syllabary

The syllabary in use. (Note the appearance of Halley's comet in the second line of the Djuka text.)

Vah, Bassa Script

The written script the Bassa people call *Vah* means "to throw a sign." (This is not to be confused with the Vai people of West Afrika, who also have their own written script called *Vai*.) Vah was initially the throwing, or making, of signs in the natural environment by chewing leaves or carving tree bark. These natural markers, or messages, were left in set locations where those for whom they were intended knew to look and how to read the marks. Eventually this communication system evolved into a complex written language. Use of the Vah script allowed Bassa people to avoid slave traders. Colonial forces halted use of the script, and the written form of the Bassa language declined almost to extinction.

The script's resurgence began in 1900 when a Liberian chemist, Thomas Gbianvoodeh Lewis (also known as Dr. Flo Darvin Lewis), discovered former Bassa slaves in Brazil and the West Indies who kept the tradition of Vah writing alive, passing it from generation to generation. Dr. Lewis brought the Bassa alphabet back to Liberia and set up schools to teach it, establishing an institution for learning Vah. Among his students were former Senator Edwin A. Morgan, and Counselors Zacharia Roberts and Jacob Logan. He also commissioned the first-ever printing press for material written in the Bassa alphabet. The revival of the Bassas' Vah script continues today with the efforts of the Bassa Vah Association (www.ie-inc.com/vkarmo/bassa.htm), striving to expand the use of this Afrikan alphabet for the printing of newspapers, literature, science, and religious texts.

Mask *Nah Wede*, Bassa, Liberia
Wood
6 x 9 x 3.5 inches
(15.2 x 22.9 x 8.9 cm)
While the Bassa *nah wede* mask bears a strong resemblance to the human face and has an aura of serenity, it represents a lively ancestral spirit who is often dubbed "the country devil." Typically, the mask has heavy lidded eyes, a small expressive mouth, and an elaborate coiffure. The coiffure has five to seven lobes above a sharply angular brow.

Courtesy the African Art Museum of the SMA Fathers, Tenafly, NJ
Gift of Dr. Richard Robertiello, 1998
Photo: Tapiwa Muronda

The Bassa Vah Alphabet

In the 1900s, Dr. Thomas Gbianvoodeh Lewis found former slaves of Bassa origin living in Brazil and the West Indies who were still using this alphabet. Dr. Lewis, himself a Bassa, had not known of the writing system and, after teaching himself to use it, revived it in Liberia, where he set up a school to teach the alphabet.

Bassa is a tonal language spoken mainly in Liberia by about 300,000 people. Tones are marked using a system of phonetic signs which appear inside the vowel letters.

Bassa (Vah) Alphabet

Signs for the Bassa Vah Tones

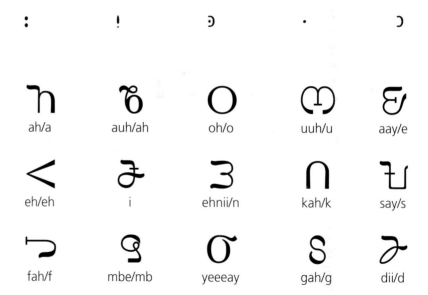

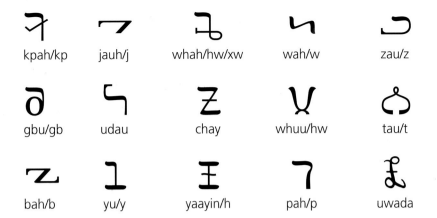

Bassa (Vah) Alphabet

kpah/kp jauh/j whah/hw/xw wah/w zau/z

gbu/gb udau chay whuu/hw tau/t

bah/b yu/y yaayin/h pah/p uwada

Bassa Tones:

	a	au	o	u	e	eh	i
high							
grave							
mid-low							
drag							
double							

125

Contemporary Alphabets

Afrikan alphabets continue to be created. Over the last 50 years, most have been developed by individuals. Most, in style and concept, rely on Afrikan cultural symbols.

Some, like the Somali script, have been adopted by government as a formal means of communication.

Some have never been in general use, and for some the detailed story of their derivation has been forgotten.

Many were created for a specific artistic or literary purpose, or as an intellectual amusement for the creator. Since 1920, there have been a wave of alphabets devised by Liberian poets and artists and other West Afrikans. Some of these alphabets are devised for writing down existing spoken languages and others are intended for personal, artistic uses. Others are revealed, often in dreams, to their inventors.

Finally mixed into this pot-pourri of modernity are some alphabets designed by my students at the Zimbabwe Institute of Vigital Arts. These are Latin alphabets, but they have an Afrikan flavor, and help to form a bridge between an Afrikan aesthetic and the European.

The Somali Script

A way with words is highly valued among the eight million Somalis. A person is judged more by linguistic dexterity than by any other quality. In Somalia, oral poetry is an art. The ability to create and recite verse elevates one's status in society.

There is a single Somali language – part of the group of languages called Eastern Cushitic that is spoken by people in neighboring Ethiopia, Djibouti, and Kenya. There are several dialects, including Common Somali (the official language used in radio and television broadcasts); but the dialects are similar enough that Somali speakers understand each other easily. Ever since independence in 1960, the Somalis have considered Somali to be the national language, but that could not be a reality until there was a nationally accepted script. This took place in 1973 and used the Latin alphabet.

Before the government introduced the Somali script in 1973, English, Italian, and Arabic were the official languages. Only English-speakers could get jobs in government and industry before 1973. This created animosity among non-English-speakers – those who could read, write, and speak Italian or Arabic as well as the many Somalis who could not read and write in any of the official languages. Once the Somali script was introduced, books on many different topics were written in the Somali language. This led to a rapid growth of literacy. It took more than a decade for there to be a substantial enough Somali literature to conduct university courses in the Somali language. By 1985 Somali had superseded English and Arabic in higher education.

The Somali Alphabet

The Somali or Osmaniya alphabet was created in 1922 by Cismaan Kenadiid, brother of the Sultan of Obbia. It has never been widely used, apart from private correspondence. The alphabet is written from left to right in horizontal rows and the letters are based on Arabic letter names. Somali is a Cushic language with over 8 million speakers in Somalia, Ethiopia, Djibouti, Kenya, Yemen, the UAE, Saudi Arabia, Italy, Finland, Sweden, and the UK. Since 1972 Somali has been written with the Latin alphabet, using orthography created by the Somali government.

Somali Alphabet

The Wolof Alphabet

Wolof is the principal language of Senegal where it is spoken by about 3.5 million people. Assane Faye, a Senegalese artist noted for his work using recycled materials, created this alphabet in 1961. The alphabet is written from right to left and is reminiscent of Arabic in its graphic style and vowel usage.

Wolof Alphabet

ay	w	y	a
c	l	t	eh
m	g	r	e
k	ng	ny	ö
b	v	f	i
mb	d	n	ah
j	nd	p	o
nj	x		u
s	ḣ		schwa
			ii

The Manenka N'Ko Alphabet

This alphabet appears to have been invented in the late 1940's or early 1950's by Souleymane Kantè of Kankan, who traveled widely in West Africa as a trader. A Muslim, and literate in both French and Arabic, Kantè named the alphabet N'ko, from the common form denoting "I say" in all the Manding dialects.

The N'ko alphabet has a total of 18 consonants, 7 vowels, and 8 diacritics (one to indicate nasal sounds and the remainder to indicate variations of vowel length and tone). Additional diacritics are used to form foreign letters wherever these are required for the transcription of words or names from other languages (European, Arabic, or African).

Writing is from right to left; characters within each word are written continuously. A series of 10 numerals employed in a decimal system is written with the lowest place of numeral on the left (in contrast to Arabic numerals).

N'Ko is used to write Mandekan, a member of the Mande group of Niger-Congo languages spoken by about 5 million people in Mali, Senegal, Guinea, Côte d'Ivoire, Burkina Faso, and Sierra Leone. Mandekan, which is also known as Manding or Mandingo, is actually a group of closely related dialects, including Bambara and Dyula, which some linguists classify as separate languages.

N'Ko Alphabet

aw	o	uh	eh	e	a	ah
m	l	k	r	d	ch	j	t	p	b
ng	y	w	h	n	ny	f	gb	s	rr

N'Ko Numerals

9	8	7	6	5	4	3	2	1	0

131

The Fula Alphabet

Devised by Adama Ba of Mali, circa 1963. It was used to write poetry and for correspondence with his friends.

Fula Alphabet

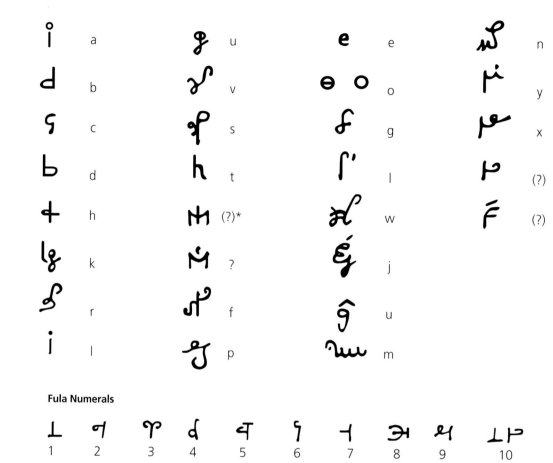

Fula Numerals

1	2	3	4	5	6	7	8	9	10

* character is recognized but its transliteration is unclear or a duplication of another sign.

The Fula Dita Alphabet

Devised by Oumar Dembele and in use between 1958 and 1966. He argued that the Fula had their own form of writing before the coming of the Arabs. He designed the alphabet based on traditional graphic symbols.

Fula Dita Alphabet

T [Ƴ] d	g	d	z
nhg	q	j	c
ah	l [ ]	w	p
o	i [ᴅ]	m [ᵛ]	x
u [ ]	u [ ]	s	bh
h	n	k	nd
t	eh	r	?
y	ny	ny	mb [ ]
a [ ]	b	f	nj
ny	e [ ]	v [ ]	

Fula Dita Numerals

1	2	3	4	5	6	7	8	9	10

133

Frédéric Bruly Bouabré and the Bété Script

In 1952 Côte d'Ivoire artist Bruly Bouabré found small red and white stones near a village called Bekora in Bété country. These stones were very varied and bore geometric drawings. He concluded that these designs were part of an ancient writing system which he called the Ivoirian alphabet, and the basis for a universal syllabic alphabet that reproduces all human sounds. In referring to this work he once said: "I drew without being the draughtsman." It is this mystical, historically grounded, yet worldly and universal quality that Bouabré projects in his drawings.

Bété Alphabet

The Bété alphabet is phonetic and contains over 400 pictograms. Shown below is a selection of the signs (some given with a transliteration and origin) to give an idea of the variety and vitality of the system. Symbols A, Ba, Bri-Bli and Bha are shown on page 136 as Bruly-Bouabré's original color drawings.

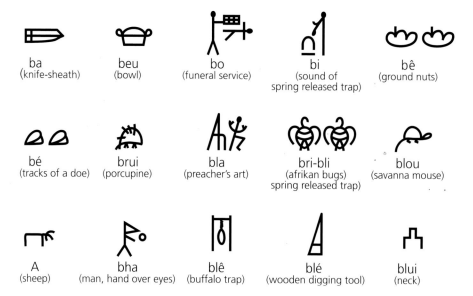

ba
(knife-sheath)

beu
(bowl)

bo
(funeral service)

bi
(sound of
spring released trap)

bê
(ground nuts)

bé
(tracks of a doe)

brui
(porcupine)

bla
(preacher's art)

bri-bli
(afrikan bugs)
spring released trap)

blou
(savanna mouse)

A
(sheep)

bha
(man, hand over eyes)

blê
(buffalo trap)

blé
(wooden digging tool)

blui
(neck)

Bété Alphabet

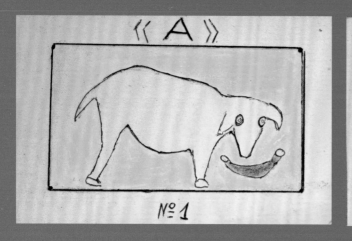

«A»

Nº 1

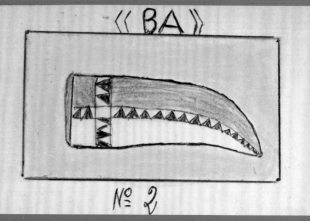

«BA»

Nº 2

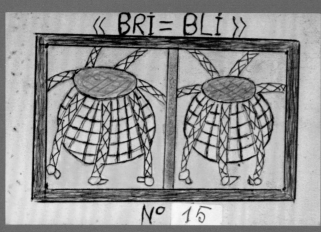

«BRI = BLI»

Nº 15

«BHA?»

Nº 26

Bouabré's art incorporates symbols and sounds from his Bété writing system. Shown on this page are 4 details from *Alphabet Bété* (1990-1991), consisting of 449 drawings.

"A" 1990 (above left)
Ballpoint pen and crayon on cardboard
3.75 x 6 inches (9.5 x 15 cm)

"BRI-BLI" 1991 (below left)
Ballpoint pen and crayon on cardboard
3.75 x 6 inches (9.5 x 15 cm)

"BA" 1991 (above right)
Ballpoint pen and crayon on cardboard
3.75 x 6 inches (9.5 x 15 cm)

"BHA" 1991 (below right)
Ballpoint pen and crayon on cardboard
6 x 3.75 inches (15 x 9.5 cm)

The Gola

Not much is known about the Gola alphabet except that it contains the 35 letters shown below and that it is likely to have been influenced by older writing systems.

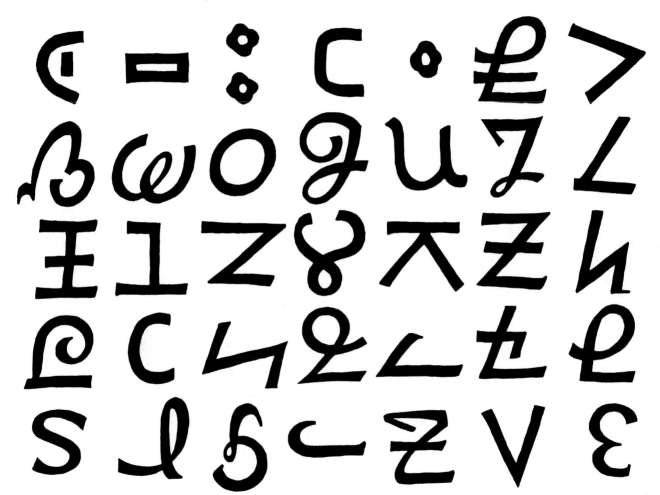

ZIVA Students

In 1998, after 18 years studying and working in the United States, I moved back home to found the Zimbabwe Institute of Vigital Arts (ZIVA) – a graphic design and new media training college. The main mission of the college – besides imparting digital design skills – is to teach students to look first to their own Afrikan culture for inspiration rather than to the West. Over the five years that the college has operated, the classes have done some interesting work in alphabet design. As a start, students work with the Roman alphabet, designing Afrikan-influenced letters. The hope is that this experience whets their appetite to do more experimental work in the field of typography.

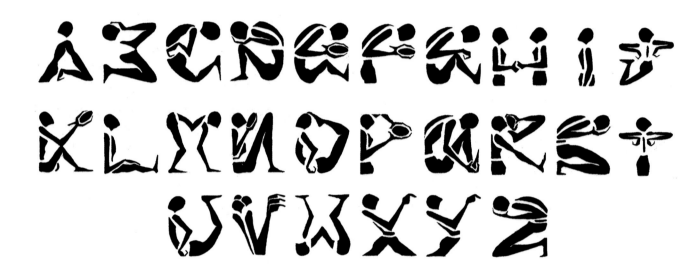

Kukumbila kunyata
(Drinking is bad for you)
Pascal Mbouti, Mozambique
UNESCO Workshop, Makerere
University, Kampala, Uganda
1999

Kaloli
(Maribou Storks)
Lilian Osanjo, Kenya
UNESCO Workshop,
Makerere University, Kampala, Uganda
1999

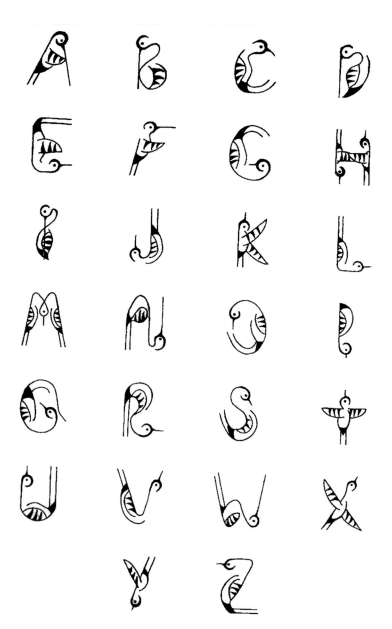

Bird Alphabet
Ryan Rodrigues
ZIVA student
2001

Rock Art Alphabet
Hailey Rogers
ZIVA student
2001

Conclusion

*i*t's been a long and difficult journey to get to where we are today as Afrikans, both at home and in the Diaspora. The primary alphabets Afrika shares with other continents – Roman and Arabic – can be expanded to incorporate the many languages of Afrikans. The vast richness of Afrikan languages can be captured in alphabets like those in this book and in others to be invented. I hope this book will be an inspiration and a guide to those who love the languages and the cultures that make our continent great.

Running ZIVA, the college I founded, has been a humbling experience. We have failed to secure funding due to the worsening political situation in my country. The economy has fallen from among the strongest in Afrika to one of the world's worst which has made operation extremely difficult. We have survived by a combination of sheer willpower, committed parents and staff, and goodwill from individuals in other parts of the globe. I have learned that very powerful work can be produced using very limited means. The emphasis is on developing creativity rather than teaching computer skills or proficiency in this or that software package. One of my biggest disappointments so far has been our failure to set up a scholarship fund since the number of have-nots far outnumbers the haves who are able to pay our fees.

On my travels and lectures abroad the big question is always, "How and where do you find teachers?" The answer to that question, I guess, offers a glimpse into the power of a good idea. We have never advertised for teachers. All our teachers are generous local business owners, not driven by the need of a high salary, which we can't afford to pay. They work with us because they believe in the cause. Globally, folks have found us on the web, and some of these have come and held workshops while others have donated much-needed hardware and software. We have also partnered with a local NGO (Non-Governmental Organization) which has provided us with hardware in return for design work. This is true Afrikan spirit, the communal village I refer to in my acknowledgements.

For Afrika to develop, there has to be a reversal of the brain drain. We have to get our brightest minds (most of whom are in the capitals of the West) back home. This is a tall order under current conditions on the continent. We have seen huge numbers of these bright minds come home, only to be so frustrated by their governments that they return to the cold climes completely disillusioned; some vowing never to return. Afrikan leaders have to provide opportunities that are conducive to the reversal of the brain drain. I am always touched by academics, like Professor Maurice Tadadjeu, who were educated at major universities in the United States and decided to return home to help rebuild Afrika. Those of us already on the continent and committed to the rebuilding process can only get stronger by networking. It is the only way, I feel, that real progress can be made. My travels on the continent have brought me to the conclusion that the ZIVA experiment can be replicated in most countries or regions.

Most Afrikan people have been surprised by my interest in their culture – but then again, that was colonization's biggest coup: to divide us into distinct groups that feel no kinship with one other. In Cameroon there is a measure of indifference to Shü-mom, King Njoya's legacy. The average Cameroonian couldn't care less. To be fair, Cameroonians are aware of their alphabet; I just got the feeling that the historical implications of this work is not fully appreciated. I have come to view the achievements of the 19th-century inventor of the Shü-mom syllabary, King Ibrahim Njoya, in the global Afrikan context rather than just simply Cameroonian. His son proposed setting up a learning center that would continue the work of his father before him; but without funding, the project has been sitting in limbo for decades.

It is up to us Afrikans ourselves to fund such projects. It is in the interests of our future that this be done. Where would the money come from? It has to start with the leadership of Afrika. Most leaders do not have the interests of their citizens at heart. There is a penchant for lavish living among our leaders. If all the money transferred to Swiss bank accounts could be repatriated, projects like this would be easily funded. Nigeria is a good example of unjust and inequitable distribution of wealth. The country rakes in billions

conversation

unity

greatness

from the exploitation of its vast oil resources, but only a few (those in power) reap the rewards. The masses languish in abject poverty, mired in a vicious cycle for survival. Isn't it ironic that although Nigeria has vast oil resources, every drop of fuel used in the country is imported! The paradoxes of my beloved continent abound!

While in Douala, Cameroon, I discovered that the people who speak Douala, the language, are Bantu and originated in the Rift Valley in Tanzania and Kenya, which is where my people, the Shona, came from. I wasn't aware that the Bantu had gone this far west! I thought the Bantu moved only southward. I heard my hosts refer to meat as *nyama*, the exact same word we Shona use in Zimbabwe thousands of miles away. Although we were unable to communicate eloquently because of my poor French, we reveled in the knowledge that we were connected through our Bantu roots. I really wish that there was more unity among Afrikans. The artificial boundaries imposed by foreign colonization are much weaker than the ties that actually bind us.

The recently formed Afrikan Union should not turn out to be what critics are accusing it of: a "toothless dog" organization that will never agree on anything or achieve anything. For the universal good of the continent's citizens there is ample opportunity for the Afrikan Union to remove the oppressive barriers imposed by colonizing powers. I suggest, as a first step, the removal of all visa requirements for Afrikans. This would make travel easier between countries, thereby promoting a better understanding of one another's cultures. Pride in our beautiful continent will follow; leading, I hope, to the "freeing of the mind" I spoke about in the introduction. As I was putting the final touches to this manuscript a Nigerian friend applied for a visa to come to Harare for a short visit. The Zimbabwean Immigration Visa Section denied her application! No reasons were given, but I was told I could appeal the decision if I wanted to. If I wanted to? Do these people know who they are dealing with here! I wrote them a scathing appeal pointing out the irony of laws that were imposed on us by Europeans who themselves have done away with them through the formation of the European Union which has scraped all visa requirements for members of the Union! I pointed out to them that I have never been denied a visa by any country anywhere on this planet and that I felt ashamed that my own country would deny a Nigerian friend entry when my application for a Nigerian visa was granted in a day! This is what the mighty Fela referred to in song as "Colo-mentality" as in colonial mentality. It IS a disease worse than "Yellow Fever" – another Fela song! The visa was issued only after I appealed in person to the chief immigration officer.

The Union should also have the authority to act against member states that have strayed from the guidelines of good governance and stability. Afrikans must learn to solve their own problems, and the leadership must be open to constructive criticism.

It is my humble hope that this book will be an eye-opener to both Afrikans and the world in general; that it will fire-up the curiosity of young Afrikans to view this work not as an end, but as a launching pad for more research and invention. There has been some work done, but we have only scratched the veneer; much more lies beneath the parched surfaces of the Afrikan deserts, and beneath the lush undergrowth of the rain forests and the grasslands of the savanna. The rocky outcrops, the hills, and the mountain ranges have enshrined in their time-weathered exteriors many stories and mysteries – all awaiting discovery.

I look forward to the glorious day when young Afrikans can read and write their own languages in Afrikan writing systems; when others (from the five corners of the globe) will accept Afrika at the table of humanity's achievements; when young Afrikans can sit proudly at this table not with eyes cast down, but with the same confidence that their peers exude. Equals. I look forward to the day when we can write about our beloved continent without having to overly explain ourselves – when our theses are accepted as fact and as a source of knowledge, not regarded with the skepticism we currently have to face. When the name *Afrika* evokes dignity, achievement, and pride, and not unrest, disease, and strife. The vast richness of Afrikan languages can be captured in alphabets like those in this book and in others to be invented. The primary alphabets Afrika shares with other continents – Roman and Arabic – can be expanded to incorporate the languages of Afrikans. I hope this book will be an inspiration and a guide to those who love the languages and the cultures that make our continent great.

A luta continua!

words

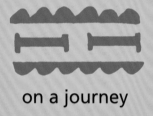

on a journey

learn from the past

Acknowledgements

ooks like this one, covering one ocean, two decades, and three continents, take many friends and colleagues to complete. My journey began with my great mentor at Yale University, Alvin Eisenman, now retired from his long tenure as the head of the Graphic Design department at the Yale School of Art. Alvin is a walking encyclopedia, well versed in a myriad of design facts and general knowledge. He got me started thinking about alphabets in the specifically Afrikan way that inspired me to write a whole book about my search. Alvin planted the seed. The late Bradbury Thompson, one of America's foremost designers and a long-time Yale professor, fostered in me a love for bookmaking. The great American designer and another Yale educator, the late Paul Rand, read my MFA thesis and encouraged me to take it further.

Karen Covington was the first editor to read the manuscript, and her sensitive and rigorous editing helped me stay focused on the Alphabets.

A big "merci beaucoup" to Marie-Laure Edom Mafundikwa who found the time to translate a couple of the texts from French.

I had tried for years, unsuccessfully, to get this book published; until my good friend John Berry, author and designer, introduced me to his friend, Mark Batty, a fledgling publisher of books on the graphic arts. I have always envisioned a stunning book, Mark's trademark is relatively small-run but beautifully produced books, and he promised no less for *Afrikan Alphabets*. I felt that at last, my story would be told with the dignity it deserves.

Journalists

"A people without a knowledge of their past is like a tree without roots." So said the great Jamaican leader Marcus Garvey. I was fortunate in my travels to meet many journalists like Michele Esso, a cousin of my New York friend Francis Mbappe, who writes for the daily newspaper in Yaoundé, Cameroon and is very knowledgeable about the Bamum. She imparted great knowledge about the Bamum people and made my stay there pleasant.

Michele Esso and son at home, Yaoundé, Cameroon.
January, 2003

Another journalist in southern Nigeria who helped me on my quest was Ms. Glory Odigha, who graciously took me around Calabar. She is a reporter and producer at a local television station, and she told me that a few months back she had done a piece on the Efik, who insist that their requirement of secrecy has led to gross misinformation and misunderstanding about their society.

The Bamum syllabary was widely thought to be extinct. Then, one fateful day, on October 21, 1997, an article by Howard W. French: "Inheritors of an African Kingdom, Come and Gone" appeared in the international section of the *New York Times*. In it I discovered that the syllabary was alive and well. Howard graciously shared his contacts. He led me to Professor Maurice Tadadjeu. *New York Times* reporter John Darnton shared his memories about his tour of duty in Lagos.

Academics

As a typographer I have learned much about linguistics and the politics of language. I was honored to have Professor Maurice Tadadjeu, a Ph.D. in Linguistics from the University of Southern California, Los Angeles, complement my work with his own. Professor Tadadjeu has been on the staff of the Department of African Languages and Linguistics at the University of Yaoundé (Cameroon) since September 1977. He served as head of Department of Language and Linguistics Research at the Yaoundé Institute of Social Sciences from 1980 to 1991, and also served as Head of Department of African Languages and Linguistics from 1993 to 1997. He is currently chair-

Professor Emmanuel Matateyou
Yaoundé University, Cameroon.
January, 2003

man of the National Association of Cameroon Language Committees (NACALCO), a federation of over 74 local language development associations. He founded the PROPELCA Project that since 1978 has developed a program for mother-tongue education in Cameroon, using a model of functional trilingual education. He has published extensively on language planning and mother-tongue education. In 1998 he initiated the project BASAL (Basic Standardization of All unwritten African Languages) intended to provide every unwritten Afrikan language with a minimum standard written form within the next 15 years. As I watch his grand scale of scholarship, I am grateful that there is a man whose vision is as large as Afrika's potential.

Professor Emmanuel Matateyou, a Bamum from Foumban, Cameroon, is an expert on Shü-mom and a linguistics professor at Yaoundé University. He wrote a letter of introduction for me to Oumarou Nchare, the Director of Cultural Affairs at the Bamum Royal Palace. I was graciously welcomed by Mr. Nchare at the Bamum Palace. He is one of the few people who know Shü-mom (at age twelve he was a Shü-mom apprentice to the current King's father, the late King Seidou Njimoluh Njoya) and he continues to teach Shü-mom at the Royal school.

I was referred to some academics like Amanda Carlson, Ph.D., University of Indiana, whose thesis was on Nsibidi, and Muneera Spence, MFA, Graphic Design, Yale, who shared their research. Other academics I know by their immense contribution to Afrikan-American studies and Afrocentric research. My work has been inspired deeply by the work of John Henrik Clarke, who set up the Black Studies department at Cornell University, where the library was named in his honor by his colleagues at the Africana Studies & Research Center. Molefe Kete Asante, chair of the Department of African-American Studies, Temple University, is the author of *Afrocentricity*. Dr. Theophile Obenga at San Francisco State University has worked with Cheikh Anta Diop and is the author of many books on Afrikan history. I have also followed, with interest, the rise of younger academics like Henry-Louis Gates at Harvard, Cornell West at Princeton, and Manthia Diawara at New York University.

Authors

Some promoters of Afrikan history, alphabets, and culture, I have not met in person, but feel I know them from their books – David Dalby, and Simon Battestini, and one I have met Robert Farris Thompson, all non-Afrikans, have dedicated their careers to bringing Afrikan languages, arts, and religions the international respect and recognition they deserve. The work of these men has proved to be an invaluable resource.

Credo Mutwa's life and work are reflected in his outstanding book, *Indaba, My Children*. This book holds important information about what he calls Bantu symbol writing systems in southern Afrika.

Malidoma Somé of Burkina Faso, in his incredible book, *Of Water and the Spirit*, recounts his abduction as a small boy by a French priest and education at a mission where he was systematically whitewashed to become Westernized. In a section that I find relevant to this book, he explains how the village elders viewed him with suspicion because he had acquired the ways of the white man – mostly the ability to write. The elders all soon come to him though, to write letters to send to sons who had left for the city looking for employment and "a better life."

Along the way I read the words of Albertine Gaur, a British author and historian, that had particular meaning to my work. She dismissed the notion of whether any form of communication can be "primitive." "Primitive" has been a term applied dismissively to Afrikan and other non-western writing systems. She writes in her excellent book *A History of Writing,* "There are no primitive scripts, no forerunners of writing, no transitional scripts as such (terms frequently used in books dealing with the history of writing), but only societies at a particular level of economic and social development using certain forms of information storage. If a form of information storage fulfills its purpose as far as a particular society is concerned then it is (for this particular society) 'proper writing.'" Gaur's is the only book that addresses the question of women's role and contribution: "Whenever the ability to write was associated with power and influence, women were, as a rule, excluded." ... "Indeed until very recently the belief prevailed (and is still not far from the surface in rural areas) that disaster would befall the family if a woman so much as held a book or pen in her hand." I hope a book on this important topic is written soon – by a woman – and an Afrikan woman would provide a view from the Afrikan perspective.

Museums

I met some amazing men and women who are dedicated to the preservation of our Afrika's past. Pascall Taruvinga, an archeologist at the **Zimbabwe Museum of Human Sciences,** shared scholarship on the Rock Art of the San. He revealed that the preferred term for them was *Hunters and Gatherers* rather than *San*. San he explained was no different from the derogatory oft-used term *bushman*. My gratitude extends to the other staff members at the **Zimbabwe Museum of Human Sciences**, especially Solomon Goredema, who stressed the need for thorough investigation rather than relying on whatever is available in published works. This field is quite dynamic, and new discoveries often render the accepted scholarship invalid.

The **Bamum Palace Museum** occupies the three main floors of the Bamum Palace in Foumban, Cameroon. The collection is huge and impressive in scope – 8,000 manuscripts. I was given permission to use images from their collection for this book.

Nath Mayo Adediran, curator at the **Calabar Museum** in Calabar, Nigeria, put together an incredible slavery exhibition. He gave me a contact that turned out to be extremely helpful.

In the United States I was helped by the generosity of the following curators who offered their time and extensive knowledge of their collections and their networks in the field of Afrikan art. Robert J. Koenig, Director of the **African Art Museum of the SMA (Societas Missionum ad Afros) Fathers** in Tenafly, New Jersey, allowed me to photograph some of the illustrations in this book from the museum's collection. Jerome Vogel at the **Museum for African Art**, New York City, assisted me with many useful contacts for needed illustrations.

Nath Mayo Adediran, curator of the Calabar Museum.
Calabar, Nigeria
January, 2003

Galleries

Skoto of **Skoto Gallery** in New York City, pointed me in the direction of contemporary artists using Afrikan alphabets in their work. It was at his gallery that I met Femi Bankole Onsula, Fela's photographer, who graciously allowed use of his photography. Brian Gaisford of the **Hemingway African Gallery** in New York City allowed me to photograph some pieces for use in this book. Helen Ramasaran is an Afrikan-American sculptor who has lived and worked in Afrika and who also shared her collection of Akan gold weights and fabrics with me. Helen runs **Sankofa Art Centre,** an art school in Brooklyn.

Leaders: political, revolutionary, and otherwise

In Calabar, my contact, Chief Etubom Bassey Ekpo, was away on business in the capital city of Abuja, but he connected me with Chief Edem Duke and Chief O.E. Eyamba, both Ekpe members like Chief Bassey. The following soldiers have blazed a trail for us to follow: Mbuya Nehanda, Sekuru Kaguvi, Chief Rekayi Tangwena, ZANLA and ZIPRA, the Mau-Mau, Malcolm X, Marcus Garvey, Martin Luther King, Nelson Mandela, Robert Sobukwe, Steve Biko, Franz Fanon, Maurice Bishop, Ivan van Sertima, the Black Panther Party, Cheikh Anta Diop, Amiri Baraka, Dr. Ben, Haile Gerima.

Friends and Family

Then of course there are the many friends and family who stood by me as I completed this task. In Afrikan societies, most tasks are tackled communally. I feel like I have created a "global village" that has rallied behind this book and encouraged me to get it published. The advent of the World Wide Web has contributed immensely to the growth of this community. Total strangers from around the globe emailed me with encouragement and support for the project. This book wouldn't have been possible were it not for the following people who have all selflessly shared their scholarship, research, and/or knowledge with me.

Mama Mbappe, was extremely warm and gracious and her hospitality was truly Afrikan.
Douala, Cameroon
January, 2003

First, *nuff respect* to my parents Amai na Baba Mafundikwa who fostered a love for all things Afrikan and instilled self-pride in me from a very early age. I have had long conversations with my father, who was educated by missionaries, and learned a lot about the psyche of those "benevolent men and women of God on a civilizing mission" whose ultimate aim was the redemption of our "pagan" souls. The treatment he received from the time he was a young student through his years of teacher training and his years of service at missionary schools sounds ridiculous and even comical to me today although there was nothing funny about it way back then. I respect him for having endured all that so that he could afford to send us to school so we could achieve a better life.

Thanks go to Diabel Faye who led me to Francis Mbappe, a New York musician. Francis gave me his family's contacts in Cameroon, including his mother, Mama Mbappe, in Douala, where I discovered our common Bantu roots. Asuquo Ukpong provided me with contacts in Calabar and the Wazara family in Lagos, Nigeria, provided generous hospitality.

Artists and Musicians

The Afrikan typographer is inspired by the other arts. Our rich heritage includes the visual arts, dance, and music. I "see" typography when I listen to mbira (the thumb piano common to most Afrikan cultures) or drum music! I want to pay homage and pour libation of the most potent palm wine ever to the genius of an Afrika long destroyed by foreign forces, those ancient artists, who without having "seen" any form of foreign writing, responded to the same stimuli that have driven humanity in other parts of the world throughout history to come up with their own forms of writing. The following artists and musicians have influenced my development as both an artist and as a proud Afrikan: the Wailers – Bob Marley, Peter Tosh, and Bunny Wailer; all the Mississippi Delta bluesmen and women. All the black musicians who created Rock 'n' Roll and Jazz, Jimi Hendrix, Miles Davis, Louise Bennett, Mutabaruka, King Tubby, Gil Scot-Heron, the Last Poets, Thomas Mapfumo, Marvin Gaye, James Brown, Stevie Wonder,

An mbira from the Tonga people of Binga in the Zambaezi Valley, Zimbabwe

Professor Longhair, the Neville Brothers, Richard Pryor, Amos Totuola, C.L.R. James, Richard Wright, Dambudzo Marechera, Tom Feelings, Jacob Lawrence, the Harlem Renaissance, Spike Lee, Boogiedown Productions, Public Enemy, Los Van Van, Celia Cruz, Fania All Stars, Afrikando.

Special thanks to those responsible for the exquisite illustrations in this book: ZIVA students Tichaona Tongoona, Christopher Masonga, and Chesterfield Mangwanya; Cynthia Batty; Faisal Naqvi; Todd Thille; Niffer Desmond; Jim Charles; True; Thea Kluge and Sebastian Schaub.

Extra special thanks go to Jason Glavy of Glavy Fonts in Nagoya, Japan, whose digitized Afrikan fonts I used in this book, and Daniel Kai of Xenotype, Seattle, Washington, who helped turn Jason's PC fonts into MacIntosh-friendly fonts.

Finally, but not in anyway least, the global family (you are too many to list here, but you know who you are) without whose encouragement and support, this book would not have been possible.

The Americas
North America: Munyaradzi "Munee" Mafundikwa – the *Next* generation, Rastaman Nasio Fontaine, Alf Muronda, Danny Dawson, Rashida Ismaili, Jocelyn Candy Cordice, Sylvia Harris, Michele Washington, Margaret Morton, Dean Robert Rindler, The Cooper Union, Ida Wood, Stacey Gemmil, Jackie McGuire, Sheila de Bretteville, Anne Dutlinger, John Obert, Jim Reidhaar, Jennifer Sonderby, Max Kisman, Alphonso Alvarez and Melanie Curry, April Banks, Ricardo Gomes, Michael Chinyamurindi, Fo Wilson, Ben Mapp, Gregory Thomson – my lawyer!, Eileen Gunn, Charlotte Sheedy Agency, Neeti Madan, Adrian Ingram, Carol Taylor, Ted Pettus, Keith Lockhart, Monica Hudson, Gauhna Singho, Gregory Bruce, Tapiwa Muronda, Connie Harvey, Alex Lindsay, Yvonne Lee Healy, Sis Jacque Kamba Omonike Geadeau, Andres Cathalifaud, Sherry Blankenship, Sam Musora, Shabaka, Jeana Aquadro, Sue Nielson, Christopher Thomas, Ivan Vhera, Owen Ndlovu, Alberto Vitalli, Fabrizzio La Rocca, Tom Russell, Janet Odgis, Banu Baker and Wilfredo Diaz.

156

South America
Colombia: Maria Camacho, Juan Salamanca and Grupo Niche.

Afrika
Cameroon: Maimounatou Bilkissou.
Nigeria: Nana Euba.
South Afrika: Chris Kabwato and family, Itumeleng Kgomo, Peter Nyaboko, Jacques Lange, Ian Sutherland and Marcus Neustetter.
Zimbabwe: The Mafundikwa posse specifically Newman, Zeff and Eunice, Mushakabvu naMai Lawrence Chaza, Muningina Chikonzero, Tendai Matemayi Tavengwa, Tanga wekwa Sando, Cuthbert Chiromo, Tafadzwa Ruziwa for holding the fort the numerous times I was away from ZIVA, ZIVA staff and students.

Caribbean
Jamaica: Harclyde and Kim Walcott, Neville Garrick.
Cuba: Leonard and Mwayemura Mandizha, Alexis Gelabert, Daniel Torralbas, Salvador, Gisele Arandea, Felipe Garcia Villamil, all the artists and the Afrikan spirits who refuse to die.

Europe
UK: Teal Triggs, Kojo Boateng, Joel Karnmarth, Eugenia Chaza, Chartwell Dutiro and Jackie Guille.
France: Joel Edom, Sylvia Edom, Michel Bouvet, Michel Olivier, Guillaume Frauly of *Étapes Graphique* Magazine and Marc Borgers.
Belgium: Jan Middendorp of Druk.
Germany: Katherina, Regula, Daniel and Mama Corsten.

Annotated Bibliography

Amin, Samir. *Eurocentrism*. London: Zed Books, 1990.

> Eurocentrism, according to Amin, is a viewpoint based on the domination of Western capitalism that claims European culture reflects a uniquely progressive position in the historical, ideological, political, and economic order of the present world. Amin provides an alternative view of world history and present-day economic and political conditions as well as a reassessment from a non-Eurocentric perspective.

Asante, Molefe Kete. *Afrocentricity*. Trenton, Africa World Press, Inc.,1988.

> Afrocentricity is a philosophical theory and curriculum model aimed at creating a collective black consciousness to engender political strength, meaningful identity, and the power necessary to positively transform the social and economic circumstances of both Afrikans and Afrikan-Americans. Speaking to blacks worldwide, Asante claims "there can be but one true objective for us in the contemporary era; to reconstruct our lives on an Afrocentric base."

Battestini, Simon. *African Writing and Text*, Brooklyn, Legas Press, 2000.

> [Translated by Professor Henri Evans from the French text published in May 1997: *Ecriture et Texte, Contribution Africaine*. Québec: Les Presses de l'Université Laval and Paris: Présence Africaine.] Battestini is a French scholar and educator who spent thirty-two years, from 1951 to 1983, studying and teaching in Afrika. His belief that no culture is without a system of conserving a common memory and communication confirmed my decision to bring Afrikan alphabets the respect they deserve. Stereotypes and myths created to justify the colonial enterprise are refuted.

Bekerie, Ayele. *Ethiopic, An African Writing System*. Trenton: Red Sea Press,1997.

> Linguistic publication about Ge'ez.
> Dr. Bekerie's book is a comprehensive study by a Western-educated Ethiopian scholar that discusses the issue of indigenous Ethiopian history through the study of its writing system, Ethiopic. Bekerie is disturbed that most historical studies of Afrikan writing systems tend to limit languages of northeastern Afrika to a geographical consideration, making them appendages of Asian and European influences in the Middle East and Mediterranean region, rather than of Afrika. The book carries an added personal significance for the Ethiopian author, who says he has a deep commitment and determination to tell the story of his people.

Cabrera, Lydia. *Anaforuana: Ritual de Símbolos de la Iniciación en la Sociedad Secreta Abakuá.* Madrid: Ediciones R., 1975.

> Cabrera devoted her life to the study of Afrikans in Cuba and their influence on the development of Cuban folklore. Monte, forest or jungle, according to the Afro-Cuban tradition, is the place where the gods and the spirit of the Afrikan ancestors of the slaves live. Her book *El Monte* has become a bible for practitioners of Santería. She also wrote a book about the rites and traditions of the secret Abakua society, *La Sociedad Secreta Abakuá*, whose membership was limited to males. That she, a white woman, was permitted access to this knowledge speaks highly of the trust and respect she inspired among her informants.

Coulmas, Florian. *The Writing Systems of the World*. Oxford: Basil Blackwell, 1989.

Clarke, John Henrik, editor. *Marcus Garvey and the Vision of Africa*. New York: Vintage, 1974.

Courtney-Clark, Margaret. *Ndebele: The Art of an African Tribe*. New York: Rizzoli, 1986.

> The women of the South African Ndebele traditionally decorated their homes lavishly with painted geometric designs and produced intricate beadwork. Margaret Courtney-Clarke spent five years visiting the Ndebele and photographing their art.

Dalby, David. *Africa and the Written Word.* Lagos: Centre Culturel Français, 1986.

> This exhibition catalog shows the historical, cultural, and artistic origins of Afrikan writing. Professor Dalby's scholarship is extensive in the area of Afrikan languages and writing systems. His work includes other books such as *Indigenous Scripts of Liberia and Sierra Leone* (1967), and with others *A Thesaurus of African languages: A classified and annotated inventory of the spoken languages of Africa* with an appendix on their written representation. Comp. Michael Mann and David Dalby with Philip Baker, et al. London: Hans Zell, 1987. He has also published widely in academic journals.

Daniels, Peter and William Bright, editors. *The World's Writing Systems*. New York: Oxford University Press, 1996.

Diop, Cheikh Anta. *The African Origin of Civilization – Myth or Reality*. Westport: Lawrence Hill, 1974.

> There is growing evidence that most achievements previously attributed to Egypt should be credited to dark-hued peoples from the south. I would, therefore, point those interested in this topic in the direction of the groundbreaking work of Afrikan scholars like Cheikh Anta Diop, whose book is an incredible resource. Over the years, my passion and interest have always lain with the marginalized south.

Fanon, Franz. *The Wretched of the Earth*. New York: Grove Press, 1963.

Faris, James. *Nuba Personal Art.* London: Gerald Duckworth & Company Limited,1972.

James, C.L.R. *The Black Jacobins,* New York: Vintage, 1963.

Garlake, Peter. *The Hunter's Vision (The Prehistoric Art Of Zimbabwe).* London: British Museum Press, 1995.
> Garlake counters the early 20th-century evaluations of the Rock Art of the San with a more contemporary assessment based on a wide knowledge of Rock Art on the continent and the cultural heritage of the San peoples.

Gaur, Albertine. *A History of Writing.* London: The British Library, 1992.
> "There are no primitive scripts, no forerunners of writing, no transitional scripts as such [terms frequently used in books dealing with the history of writing], but only societies at a particular level of economic and social development using certain forms of information storage. If a form of information storage fulfills its purpose as far as a particular society is concerned then it is 'proper' writing."

Haley, Alex. *The Autobiography of Malcom X.* New York: Grove Press, 1965.

Jensen, Hans. *Sign, Symbol and Script.* New York: G.P. Putman's Sons,1969.

Lévi-Strauss, Claude. *Myth and Meaning.* New York: Schocken Books,1979.

Meggs, Philip, B. *A History of Graphic Design,* Second Edition, Van Nostrand Reinhold,1992.

Mutwa, Vusamazulu Credo, *Indaba, My Children: African Tribal History, Legends, Customs and Religious Beliefs,* Edinburgh: Payback Press, 1998.
> An oral history of sub-Saharan Afrika written by Sangoma, or healer, Credo Mutwa begins with the creation story and telling of the violent co-existence of immortals and mortals, and the migration of the peoples to places they occupy today. The title means "gather round, my children" or "Once upon a time."

Nchare, Oumarou. *The Writing of King Njoya, Genesis, Evolution, Use.* Foumban: Palais des Roi Bamoun, Maison de la Culture.

Ong, Walter J. *Orality and Literacy: The Technologizing of the World.* London: Methuen, 1982.

Onor, Sandy Ojang. *The Ejagham Nation in the Cross River Region of Nigeria,* Ibadan: Kraft Books Limited, 1994.

Scribner, Sylvia, and Michael Cole. *The Psychology of Literacy,* Cambridge: Harvard University Press, 1981.

Sertima, Ivan Van. *They Came Before Columbus.* New York: Random House, 1974.

Somé, Malidoma Patrice. *Of Water and the Spirit*. New York: Penguin Books, 1994.

Thompson, Irwin William. *The Time Falling Bodies Take to Light*. New York: St. Martin's Press, 1981.

Thompson, Robert Farris. *Flash of the Spirit*. New York: Vintage Books, 1983.
> The renowned art historian discusses the impact of the Yoruba, Congo, Dahomey, Cross River, and Mande Afrikan cultures on the art and religious and philosophical beliefs of people of Afrikan ancestry in the New World. A strong resource on Nsibidi writing of the Ejagham people and Anaforuana in Cuba.

Wahlman, Maude Southwell. *Signs and Symbols: African Images in African American Quilts*. Atlanta: Tinwood Books, 2001.

Zaslavsky, Claudia. *Africa Counts, Number and Pattern in African Culture*. Westport: Lawrence Hill & Company, 1979.
> A study of mathematical thinking among Afrikan peoples covers counting in words and in gestures; the measurement of time, distance, weight, and other quantities; complexities of number systems; patterns in music, poetry, art, and architecture.

Periodicals:

Darnton, John. "How Fela landed me in jail." *New York Times*: July 20, 2003.

Eakin, Emily. "Writing as Block for Asians." *New York Times*: May 3, 2003.

French, Howard W. "Inheritors of an African Kingdom Come and Gone." *New York Times*: October 21, 1997.

Newsweek, "Afrocentrism: Was Cleopatra Black?" September 23, 1991.

Thompson, Robert Farris, "Black Ideographic Writing: Calabar to Cuba," Yale Alumni Magazine 42.2: 29–33, 1978.

Web Sites:

www.ethnologue.com
> Ethnologue.com is a place to find many resources related to the world's languages. Owned by SIL International, it is a service organization that works with people who speak the world's lesser-known languages. The language data you will find on this site came from the Ethnologue database.

www.geocities.com/nko_alpha
> N'Ko alphabet sources are found here, including a biography of its creator and the history of the use of the alphabet .

www.ie-inc.com/vkarmo/bassa.htm

The Bassa Vah Association promotes the teaching and use of the Bassa Alphabet. This site is a source of a Bassa Vah font and the history of the script.

www.jaars.org/museum/alphabet/galleries/africa.htm

The Museum of the Alphabet is a public service of JAARS (Jungle Aviation and Radio Services) Inc., which provides technical support to SIL (Sumner Institute of Languages) International. The historic work of the founding organization was Bible translation. An actual museum is located on the campus of the JAARS Center, near Waxhaw, NC. Some information on this site's Afrikan gallery conflicts with other contemporary information cited in this book about Ethiopic, Vai, Bamum.

www.library.cornell.edu/africana/Writing_Systems

On the John Hendrik Clark Library site, Professor Ayele Bekerie introduces information about Afrikan writing systems including: Ethiopic (Ge'ez), Afan-Oromo Script, Amharic Syllographs, Ethiopic System w/ Numeric Values, Bassa Script, Egyptian Writing System, Meroitic Script, Vai Syllabary, Mende Script, Nsibidi, Rock Arts, Akan weights, Adinkra symbols, Wabuti art, and Tifinagh.

www.omniglot.com

Simon Ager's website provides a guide to over 160 different alphabets, syllabaries, and other writing systems. It also contains details of many of the languages written with those writing systems and links to a wide range of language-related resources, such as fonts, online dictionaries, and online language courses.

www.quiresiste.com

Pierre di Sciullo is a French designer, author, and typographer. He digitized Tifinagh with the help of a group of Tuareg friends. His fonts are available on his website and the Tifinagh can be downloaded for free.

www.thisdayonline.com/archive

Ijeoma Oguachuba posted an article here on Nsibidi in 2003.

http://user.dtcc.edu/~berlin/font/bassa.htm

Site for alternate Bassa (Vah) font.

www.welltempered.net/adinkra

Source for Adinkera symbols and their meanings.

Glossary

alphabet
: a type of writing system that uses consonants and vowels.

character
: a mark or a sign used as a symbol in writing or printing; general term for any self-contained element of a writing system.

cicatrisation
: making permanent patterns in the flesh by cutting the skin so that healing tissue forms scars.

consonant
: a brief portion of an utterance in which obstruction to the air stream is created in the vocal tract (e.g. in English the **b** or **p** sounds made with the lips, or the **k** sound make in the back of the throat); also a character designating such a sound.

cursive
: flowing, showing the influence of the motion of hand in writing, often with joined characters.

diacritic
: a mark or a sign (such as ˜ _ ˆ ˇ) placed over, under, or through a letter to indicate pronunciation; a mark added to or combined with a character or letter to indicate a modified pronunciation such as the difference between the French **e** in *résumé* and in *Agnès*.

epigraphy	the study of inscriptions made on hard surfaces such as a monument, building, or tombstone; the study of texts inscribed on hard surfaces, usually by incising characters into stone.
glyph	an image or symbolic figure, often engraved or incised, that imparts information.
grammatology	the study of writing systems.
grapheme	a written symbol used to represent speech; unit of a writing system, a character, letter, diacritical mark, or sign.
graphic arts	the fine or applied visual arts and associated techniques in which forms are represented visually on a flat surface, especially those arts where images are produced from blocks, plates, or type, as in engraving and lithography.
ideogram	or ideograph; a written symbol that stands for an object or idea rather than for a word; a symbol that represents an idea or object directly rather than a particular word or speech sound, such as the "man" and "woman" symbols used on public restrooms that designate which is the men's or ladies' room, or the circle with a bar through it over a cigarette understood to mean "no smoking."
letter	a mark or a character, usually printed or written, that stands for one or more speech sounds; a self-contained unit of a writing system, a character, a glyph representing speech sounds.
morpheme	the smallest unit of speech; language unit that cannot be further divided into smaller parts.

mnemonic device	something intended to assist the memory and help a person remember more complex information.
orthography	the art of writing words with the proper letters according to accepted usage with correct spelling.
phonetic	of or pertaining to speech sounds, their production, or their transcription in written symbols.
phonetic alphabet	an alphabet containing a separate character for each distinguishable speech sound.
pictograph	a picture that stands for a word or idea in a system of writing; picture or sign or symbol used to record information, as in a system of picture writing.
scarification	making permanent patterns in the flesh by cutting the skin so that healing tissue forms scars.
script	a writing system or style; the glyphs, letters or characters used in writing by hand; a particular system of writing such as Nsibidi or Somali script.
syllable	a word or part of a word pronounced with a single uninterrupted sounding of the voice and the letter or group of letters used in writing or printing to represent this.
syllabary	a writing system composed of characters that represent syllables, yielding a catalog of sounds common to the language that can be combined to form the spoken words.

vowel	a voiced speech sound, or a character representing such a sound, made by not blocking the passage of air through the mouth and forming a syllable or part of a syllable; in English the characters a, e, i, o, u represent these sounds.
writing system	a method of recording language in a permanent form understandable by others and using it to convey information.

Sources:

The *American Heritage® Dictionary of the English Language*, Fourth Edition. New York: Houghton Mifflin Company, 2000.

The World's Writing Systems. Peter Daniels and William Bright, editors. New York: Oxford University Press, 1996.

Index

Colophon

This book was designed on a Macintosh iBook laptop computer. Design began in Harare, Zimbabwe, was completed in New York City, and fine-tuned in Harare. Design@7 provided FTP downloading and uploading facilities to MBP's web site.

Page layout was done in QuarkXpress 5.0, and image creation and manipulation was done in Adobe Photoshop 7.0 and Illustrator 10.

All photographs by author, except for the Cuba shots, were shot on a Fuji A303 3.2 mega pixel digital camera. The Cuba shots were shot on Fuji film on a Canon Rebel X 35mm camera.

Typefaces used for the book are as follows: Franklin Gothic for title and heads, and Frutiger for text and captions. The Afrikan fonts (*Vai, Ethiopic, Mende, Loma, Kpelle, Bassa Vah, N'Ko, Bété and Djuka*) were digitized for the PC by Jason Glavy of Glavy Fonts, Nagoya, Japan and Daniel Kai of Xenotype, Seattle made them Mac friendly.

There is a deluxe edition of 20 copies, and a special edition of 60 copies that are hand-bound and slipcased with special examples of Afrikan alphabets in use.

Epilogue

Ngomakurira Mountain, near Harare, Zimbabwe and west of the Domboshava Cave, boasts its own impressive Rock art. Tichakunda and Simba play digital games in front of a magnificent painting that dates from over twenty thousand years ago. The sound effects of their Gameboys contrast starkly to the natural sounds deep in the Ngomakurira (*Sound of drums playing*) cave. The juxtaposition of the new with the ancient reminds me of the modern means and methods I have used to dig up our glorious past.